THE
happy puppy
HANDBOOK

D0110231

THE
happy puppy
HANDBOOK

Your Definitive Guide to
Puppy Care and Early Training

Pippa Mattinson

EBURY
PRESS

5 7 9 10 8 6 4

Published in 2014 by Ebury Press, an imprint of Ebury Publishing

A Random House Group Company

Text copyright © Pippa Mattinson
Design copyright © Ebury Press

Picture credits:
Del Waghorn www.thedogphotographer.co.uk (with kind permission of the Wolf Conservation Trust): 13, 46; Jon Lane: 6, Julie Thorpe: 124, 138, 143 (top), 153, 163, 189; Karen Rizzo: 176; Heidrun Humphries: 105 (right); Martin Austwick: 51, 118 (bottom); Mike Cooter www.makelightwork.com: 24, 90, 109, 127, 142, 203; Nick Ridley www.nickridley. com: 2, 8, 11, 14, 21, 22, 26, 30, 32, 34, 41, 42, 49, 53, 56, 59, 60, 62, 65, 66, 72, 77, 79, 80, 81, 92, 93, 95, 97 (top), 100, 107, 110, 119, 121, 131, 134, 135, 137, 140, 143 (bottom), 146, 149, 150, 155, 156, 165, 167, 170, 172, 177, 178, 181, 185, 201, 205, 210, 214, 216; Pippa Mattinson: 29, 35, 39, 44, 67, 68, 73, 91, 94, 97 (bottom), 98, 114, 116, 122, 129, 179; Rhian White www.brightondogphotography.co.uk: 16, 84, 103, 105 (left), 118 (top), 123, 133, 207; Toby Mattinson: 37, 160, 213

The Random House Group Limited Reg. No. 954009

Addresses for companies within the Random House Group can be found at www. randomhouse.co.uk

A CIP catalogue record for this book is available from the British Library

Penguin Random House is committed to a sustainable future for our business, our readers and our planet. This book is made from Forest Stewardship Council® certified paper.

MIX
Paper from
responsible sources
FSC
www.fsc.org FSC® C018179

To buy books by your favourite authors and register for offers visit
www.randomhouse.co.uk

Printed and bound in Italy by Printer Trento S.r.l.

ISBN 9780091957261

❧ Contents

Pippa Mattinson is a zoologist and the founder of The Gundog Trust – the UK's first gundog training and welfare charity. She is a keen supporter of modern, science-based dog training methods, and is passionate about helping people to enjoy their dogs. Visit her website for more information: www.pippamattinson.com

Acknowledgements

I should like to thank all the many puppy owners around the world who have written to me, or posted questions on my websites and forum, about their puppies. It is you who are the inspiration for this book.

I should like to thank my husband Duncan for his unwavering support and enthusiasm, and my sons Toby and Tom for their encouragement. I am indebted to my daughters Sammie and Lucy, and my sister Sandra, for their thoughtful and constructive help with proofreading, and to all my family for enabling me to indulge my passion for writing and for dogs.

I should also like to thank my editor Marion Paull for her sympathetic and considered revisions, and Nicki Crossley at Ebury for her help and enthusiasm for this project. Thanks also to my agent Christopher Little, and my son-in-law Oz, for making it happen.

Finally, thanks to the scientists and authors mentioned in the references. They and many others have provided the foundations and momentum for the establishment of positive methods of raising and training puppies.

Part One

Preparing for your puppy

1

A new life

Our unique partnership with dogs is built upon ten thousand years or more of friendship and co-operation. It has weathered all the changes we have experienced together on our journey through time.

It is difficult to grasp the sheer scale of the history we share with dogs, and fascinating to consider that somewhere back in the Stone Age your own puppy's paleolithic predecessors were being embraced into human families. The depth of this association between our two species is reflected in the privileges we now allocate to our dogs and in the emotional ties we form with them.

Our relationship with the domestic dog is truly remarkable, and every new puppy represents the chance to reaffirm the bond between us.

Part of the family

The addition of a puppy to your family is a significant event and should be a wonderful experience for all concerned. Your puppy will be special and unique, a product of both his own genetic inheritance and of the loving environment you provide for him. And like every new puppy, his arrival represents the promise of a new life and shared future together.

The build-up to the day you collect your puppy will be exciting and even a little daunting. You will want to do the very best you can for him, to make sure you give him the right things to eat, and the right amount of exercise. You will also want to make good choices about your puppy's health and training. The purpose of this book is to make sure you have all the information you need to look after your puppy on a day-to-day basis, and to make those important decisions about his care. Above all, I want to help you make sure that your puppy becomes a happy and valued member of your family and of the wider community.

Hopes and dreams

Bringing a puppy into your life is not just a question of buying a new pet. It is a bigger decision than that, a much greater responsibility and opportunity. In many ways, dogs are far more than simply pets – they are an extension of our human family.

As you await the arrival of your new puppy, you will have expectations of your life together. We all want our puppies to be clean, happy, healthy and friendly. We want them to be gentle with our children and other pets. We may look forward to long walks together, games together, resting by the fire together. We hope that our puppy will come racing towards us when we whistle and that he will learn to follow basic house rules at home.

We hope our puppy will come racing towards us when we whistle.

Whilst expectations are always high, life with a puppy is not always plain sailing. New puppies are messy, untrained and can be destructive and noisy. We all know that adult dogs should be clean, obedient, quiet and well mannered. But getting from the first state to the second in the space of a few months is not inevitable, as anyone who has met an untrained and bad-mannered adult dog will tell you. Raising a good canine citizen requires the input of a willing and committed owner.

Caring for your puppy

Most people accept that they will need to invest some time and effort in realising their aspirations for their puppy. They appreciate that puppies need help to grow into well-behaved dogs. But many new dog owners are unclear about the kind of help their puppy will need, or the point at which he will need it. To complicate matters, there is a lot of confusing and conflicting advice available to new puppy owners. It can be difficult to know which way to turn. Should you dominate your puppy? Or train him with treats? Can you feed him chicken? Is it spoiling him to let him sleep on your sofa or let him eat before you? How can you be a pack leader and his friend at the same time? Are dog crates cruel, and should you teach your dog to wee on puppy pads or newspaper? There are so many questions, and so many different opinions on how to care for a puppy and how to achieve the dog of your dreams.

Throughout the next few chapters we will be building up your understanding and knowledge about how puppies learn and develop. We will look not only at the physical changes in your puppy's body over the next few months, and how to keep him healthy, but also at what goes on inside his head. By the end of this section of the book, you will know the answers to the important questions above, and to many others, too. You won't be dependent on outdated opinions to make good decisions for your puppy, or misled by the latest fads in dog care.

Natural instincts

Puppies get into a lot of trouble for simply being puppies. A great deal of that trouble can be avoided if we close the gap between what is expected of the puppy and what he is capable of. Understanding what is normal for puppies is the first step in that direction.

People have speculated and disagreed for decades on the true origins of the domestic dog, but DNA testing has finally put the debate to bed. Your puppy's ancestors were wolves, and some of the natural instincts he still carries in his genes are relics from his past and evident in his early behaviour patterns. Despite the way in which his development has been influenced by domestication, your puppy is still very much a dog. He still comes programmed with a whole bundle of instincts designed to ensure that he is fit for life as a social predator. And some of these instincts, which are perfectly acceptable in a wild-dog family, may result in behaviour that is decidedly inappropriate in our modern world. Chasing your neighbour's cat, for example, is unlikely to go down well, yet many breeds of dog are still *physically* capable of hunting down and even killing small animals.

Some of your puppy's natural instincts are actually quite useful to us. We can use his instinct for chasing moving objects to establish an excellent recall and to teach him to fetch a ball. His wolf-like instinct for keeping his den or sleeping area clean will help you to house-train him. Some puppy instincts are less helpful. Gnawing his way through the legs of your antique table, or digging up the herb garden, are rarely approved puppy pastimes, yet chewing and digging are very natural to puppies.

Your puppy's ancestors were wolves.

Just like our children, puppies need to be educated and taught that some of their most basic instincts must be kept in check. They need to learn new and often unnatural (for a dog) ways to behave. They need to be taught not to use indoor human buildings for toilet purposes, to play gently with their human friends, and to obey our commands and signals. All dogs need to be confident moving around in public places and among strangers, and to be friendly to the people they meet there.

Avoiding trouble

Whilst many puppies integrate smoothly into human society and live contented lives as well-adjusted canine citizens, some do not. If not correctly managed, puppyish behaviours may persist. What was cute in a tiny puppy may be less endearing in a muddy 80lb adult. Behavioural problems, such as aggression, running away and separation anxiety, can develop and may result in dogs facing rejection by the families who not long ago awaited their arrival with excitement. Many of the problems dog owners face have their roots in early puppyhood. The great news is that the vast majority of them can be avoided, and what cannot be avoided can usually be overcome.

Educating your puppy into more grown-up behaviour is a gradual process, and often involves redirecting him into more appropriate activities or restricting his access to your more treasured possessions. Many people get into difficulties with small puppies because they allow them too much freedom, and give them access to frequent opportunities to make bad decisions before the puppy has the self-control or knowledge to make better ones.

We can divert the chasing instinct into the retrieve.

To begin with, the vast majority of your puppy's free time will need to be controlled. Life with a puppy can quickly lose its flavour if we have to spend every waking moment saying 'No!', 'Stop it!', 'Leave that!' Just like living with a toddler, we don't want to be forever nagging at a puppy, so we make some changes around the house to reduce his opportunities for mischief. We'll look at these simple preparations in more detail later on in this section, as they will make the next few weeks a great deal easier for both of you.

Gradually, as your puppy learns what is and what is not acceptable in our human world, you will be able to give him more freedom and more choices. Over the space of just a few weeks you will see some rapid changes. Of course, there may be times when you find your puppy's behaviour challenging, or frustrating. There will be ups and downs, but with the help of this book, I hope you find the ups are many and the downs are few and far between.

🐾 A modern dog

Many of the instincts that our dogs have inherited from wolves are greatly diminished, some have been enhanced by selective breeding, and others lost completely. Puppies are much easier to befriend than wolf cubs, even when raised in identical circumstances. And dogs have become more skilful at reading and anticipating human behaviour.

In the light of recent research, a number of beliefs and understandings about the instinctive social behaviour of dogs have been revised or discarded. It is worth looking at these briefly, because they were widely held until just twenty years ago, and for many years the principles of all dog management and training were based upon them.

Wolves were understood to be pack animals that lived within a strict social hierarchy where a dominant animal held the position of leader or 'alpha' and maintained that position through physical strength and superiority. Any sign of weakness in the leader would lead to conflict and a challenge for his position of power. Dogs were believed to have inherited this social behaviour, and dog trainers believed that dogs had to be controlled and kept in their place through domination and strong pack leadership.

We now know that much of this theory was incorrect. Dogs do not tend to form packs or strict social hierarchies under normal circumstances; nor do they maintain social relationships through force or displays of dominance. Recent studies have shown that even wolves don't form packs in quite the same way that we once believed they did. The original research was based on unrelated captive wolves that had been thrust together in a most unnatural manner. More recent studies of wild wolves tell a different story, of animals that live in a close family unit, led usually by parents and maintained without aggression.

What this new research means for you is that you don't need to worry about dominating your puppy, and nor should you be concerned that he will try to dominate you. Dogs may fight over resources, such as food, but dominance is not something they value. You will achieve your rightful position as the head of your puppy's family through controlling the resources available to him as part of an effective training strategy.

The learning curve

Our two species have grown and evolved together over time. Whilst your puppy retains some echoes of his wolf ancestry, he will be very much a modern dog. And although his natural instincts may govern a lot of his early development, he also has a huge capacity to learn.

With every day that passes, your puppy's newly learned behaviours will have an increasing influence on his daily activities. Just like small children, puppies have little self-control or sense of danger, and life with a puppy can be hard work. But it should also be fun. Your puppy should fit in with *your* life, not the other way around.

Some puppies have little sense of danger.

Understanding how your puppy learns, and how you can influence that process, is the focus of our next chapter. Within that understanding lies the key to a happy and enjoyable relationship with your dog. By the time you have finished *The Happy Puppy Handbook,* you will know how to make your puppy feel at home, how to get him to sleep at night, and how to avoid him crying excessively. You will also know how to feed him and house-train him and how to keep him healthy.

But most importantly, you will know how to ensure that he grows up well adjusted and well equipped to live in harmony with all the other inhabitants of our crazy, chaotic and cluttered human world.

 SUMMARY
- Life with a new puppy can be challenging.
- Puppies need a little help to become happy and well adjusted.
- Most behavioural problems can be avoided.

2
How puppies learn

The ability of our canine friends to learn amusing tricks, and even to carry out useful tasks on our behalf, is part of their enduring appeal. We can teach dogs to herd sheep, retrieve lost items, dance to music, guide and assist their disabled owners, and even to detect total strangers buried in the rubble of an earthquake zone. Dogs are very good at learning a wide range of skills.

Teaching a puppy right from wrong ought to be straightforward enough. Yet as attitudes towards dogs have changed, there seems to be increasing confusion over how to teach our puppies what is and is not acceptable.

Dog owners may be faced with conflicting advice. Training with food or other rewards may be dismissed by traditional-style trainers as too soft or permissive, whilst traditional-style methods may be dismissed by others as too harsh.

Puppies learn very fast indeed. They learn from you and from other members of their family, but they also learn from interacting with everything else around them. We all want our puppies to 'sit' and 'come here', to 'lie down' and to 'stay'. Yet in the first few weeks in their new homes, what many puppies are learning is to 'whine' and 'jump up' and to 'snatch' and 'bark'. Fortunately, we have a great deal of control over this process, provided we understand how it happens. For great results, you need to be clear how the mechanism of the learning process actually works – preferably before your new puppy sets foot inside your home.

The three outcomes

The learning process that has evolved in dogs and other mammals is very straightforward. Inside your puppy's brain, the consequences of every single action he carries out are recorded and allocated to one of three categories. Those categories are:

- **Good** (things just got better)
- **Bad** (things just got worse)
- **Indifferent** (nothing changed)

Which of the three categories those consequences fall into will determine how your puppy will behave next time he is in the *same* situation. Let's look at some examples.

If your puppy pokes a tennis ball with his nose, it is quite likely to roll along the ground. If there is a bit of a slope, he may even get to chase after it. Things just got better for the puppy and his brain records a good consequence. Next time he sees a tennis ball, he will be likely to poke it again. On the other hand, if your puppy pokes a wasp with his nose, he may get stung, in which case things just got worse for him. A bad consequence is recorded and the puppy's brain will look out for similar situations in the future. Next time he sees a wasp he will probably leave it alone.

Timing is a crucial factor in this process. If your puppy pokes a wasp and it flies away, then returns and stings him later, he will not connect the two and will probably poke a wasp again in the future. The consequence, good or bad, must accompany the puppy's actions or follow very closely in order to have any effect.

This is all pretty obvious and applies to people, too. If what we do is followed by a bad thing, we don't do it again. If what we do is followed by a good thing, we do it more often.

But what about our third category of outcomes? What if the outcome is registered by the puppy as 'indifferent'? What happens if nothing changes? If your puppy pokes a large rock with his nose for example, rocks being what they are, he is unlikely to get a reaction. His brain adds the experience to the indifferent category.

But here is the interesting part. If there is no outcome, if nothing changes following the puppy's actions, his behaviour is less likely to occur in the future. The effect is, in fact, the same as if the puppy had been punished. If repeated, this lack of outcome results in a process called 'extinction' because over time, the behaviour that it follows will die out. Here is a summary of our three outcomes and their influence on your puppy's future behaviour.

- **Good outcome**   =   increased behaviour
- **Bad outcome**   =   diminished behaviour
- **Indifferent outcome** =   diminished behaviour

The way in which these three outcomes control your dog's future behaviour is no accident. The ability of your dog to record, and act on, the consequences of past behaviour has evolved to make sure that any behaviour that is *beneficial* to the dog will increase. Any behaviour that is not beneficial to the dog dies out, enabling the dog to preserve his time and energy for more productive activities. Puppies do what works for *them*.

Taking control

In each of the examples opposite the puppy was learning without the intervention of his owner. We often call this 'accidental learning'. In homes where puppies have a great deal of freedom, most of his learning is likely to be accidental. Raising a puppy without bad habits and with nice manners requires that we take control of the consequences of his actions to a much greater degree.

The *ways* in which we control the consequences of our puppy's actions have changed significantly in the last twenty years or so. It is worth looking at just what those changes have involved.

Traditional dog training

In behavioural science, any consequence that makes a behaviour more likely to happen again in the future is defined as a 'reinforcer'. Any consequence that makes a behaviour less likely to happen again in the future is defined as a 'punisher'. An effective punisher must be something the dog finds disagreeable, an effective reinforcer must be something the dog finds highly desirable, and both must be easy to apply. Both punishers and reinforcers need to be free from harmful side effects.

Traditional dog trainers used what they thought was a fair balance between punishment and reinforcement. Unfortunately, the principles of effective training with reinforcement were not well understood, and many dogs were not offered desirable (to the dog) rewards nor rewarded in a way that creates a trained response. We will look at this more closely in a moment. But what this lack of knowledge meant was that traditional training leant quite heavily on punishment.

People's attitudes to dogs today are very different from those of previous generations. Dogs are often considered as friends and family members, and dog owners are less inclined to punish them. Even putting to one side the ethics of using punishment, there are practical problems in its application.

Practical problems with punishment

We noted on previous pages that timing is a crucial factor in applying consequences. This can be a problem when it comes to punishment because, unsurprisingly, dogs do not like being punished. Most puppies do not hang around waiting to be smacked once they realise that you are in a bad mood. Catching and chastising a puppy where and exactly when a misdemeanour is committed is often impossible. This situation does not improve as the puppy gets older.

Regular punishment can greatly reduce a puppy's desire to be near to his owner, and this may seriously impact on the quality of his recall. Punishment also makes the punisher feel angry when he should be remaining calm in order to think objectively how best to respond to his dog. In addition, many dogs become hardened to punishment and need increasingly severe corrections to achieve the same effect. You can see how an escalating spiral of harsh treatment can creep in to spoil a previously happy relationship, often because the owner was afraid of spoiling the dog by being too soft, and didn't know what else to do.

Fortunately, times have changed and the way in which dogs learn through consequences is much better understood. Pioneering behaviourists and dog trainers have perfected positive-reinforcement techniques and transformed the way in which we now teach and manage our dogs. The movement away from punishment as a training tool is now widely established and training your puppy should be fun for both of you.

Modern dog training

The reliance that traditional trainers placed on punishment was not due to rewards being any less effective than aversives. It arose because trainers weren't using reinforcement of the right kind, and in the right way.

Effective reinforcers must be highly desirable to the *dog*. And many dogs are not overly impressed with praise and patting. Just like you and me, one dog's preference may be different from another's. If you pay me in cabbages, I am unlikely to want to work for you again. Belgian chocolates, on the other hand, would be a different matter. You might be induced to provide your expertise in exchange for a white-water rafting trip, but your neighbour would sooner work for some tickets to the theatre. In the same way, some dogs will find tug games very motivating; others might prefer opportunities to retrieve a ball. Almost all dogs are impressed by certain foods – moist and highly flavoured ones are preferred. For puppies under three months old, it is also worth remembering that one of the most powerful rewards you can offer is your attention.

Studies have shown that dogs will work very hard for food rewards, and the harder the dog is prepared to work, the quicker a trained response can be created.

Good things happen when you poke a tennis ball.

Since food is easily portable and quickly delivered, it is an ideal dog-training tool. Using other types of reward is perfectly acceptable, provided that the rewards you have in mind are genuinely desirable to the dog in question.

The most important point is that you do not have any power to make an experience in itself reinforcing for your dog. You cannot force your dog to enjoy eating cheese, chasing balls or being cuddled. Your job is to observe and recognise what *your dog* perceives as reinforcing, and this requires a degree of honesty that most of us struggle with at first. We all want to believe that our dog loves praise, cuddling and being stroked by us, more than all the world. The hard truth may be that he would rather eat roast beef or chase butterflies.

Accepting that you can train a puppy far more quickly with chicken than with cuddles is only part of the battle. You also need to apply your effective rewards in an effective way. You cannot just shovel treats down a dog indefinitely and expect to maintain his new behaviour. Many people struggle with treat-based training because they don't realise that in the long run treats must be delivered intermittently. Predictable rewards soon get boring. And bribing your puppy to be good is not the answer.

Training versus bribery

A bribe is something offered in advance in order to get the required response. If you hold out a piece of food to your puppy and ask him to sit, you are

Nowadays dogs are often considered to be family members.

offering a bribe. Bribery is a highly ineffective long-term strategy. The owner of the dog has no control when the bribe is unavailable, or when the dog has his eye on a better reward, such as running around with your best shoes or playing with another dog.

Training is quite different. Training creates an automatic behaviour that endures, even when rewards are not always available. Dogs can be trained to respond to a signal, such as coming to your recall whistle, but also to respond to being in a certain situation, such as remaining silent in a crate, or sitting politely when visitors stroke him. Training is the process by which we create or modify a behaviour through the intelligent use of rewards. And to do this well, we need to understand how animals have evolved a way to remain persistent in the face of difficulty.

Pleasurable consequences are a great way to establish new behaviour, but they do not work as reinforcers if they continue to be predictable. This is because there is an evolutionary advantage to being persistent. Nature is not always predictable. A wild-dog family may chase five or six antelope before they make a kill. If they give up after the first chase, they would starve. Persistence in the face of intermittent rewards is essential. For this reason, dogs, and other mammals such as ourselves, are programmed to find random and unpredictable rewards *more* desirable than reliable and predictable ones. This phenomenon, which has been very well studied, explains our enthusiasm for slot machines and penny-pusher fairground games. It is very aptly named the 'gambling effect'.

What this means for you is that once you have established some nice behaviours in your puppy, you will need to begin to provide rewards for them unpredictably – sometimes giving a big reward, sometimes a little one, and sometimes no reward at all. This will help you ensure that your puppy becomes addicted to good behaviour and that the behaviours you teach him become deeply ingrained.

Correcting bad behaviours

We have talked a lot about encouraging good behaviour. Positive reinforcement is a great way of training new behaviours but there are still times when puppies will behave badly. How do we stop a puppy from digging up the lawn, or jumping all over the furniture? How do we correct unwanted behaviours? Won't we still need punishment for this?

Let's go back to our three consequences again.

- Good outcome (reinforcement)　　=　　increased behaviour
- Bad outcome (punishment)　　=　　diminished behaviour
- Indifferent outcome (extinction)　　=　　diminished behaviour

So far we have looked at good and bad consequences, but we haven't paid much attention to our third consequence. You may remember that an indifferent outcome, or no consequence, diminishes the preceding behaviour in just the same way as punishment. Extinction is a powerful tool and modern dog trainers are increasingly choosing it to replace the use of punishment. This means being pro-active in the way that we manage our dogs in order to ensure that

Food is a useful training tool.

undesirable behaviours are extinguished. We need to make sure that family members do not pet the dog when he puts his feet on their laps, or feed him titbits when he begs at the table. If the puppy receives no benefit from his behaviour, he will give up fairly quickly.

You can significantly hasten this process of extinguishing naughty behaviours by rewarding an alternative behaviour to replace the one you do not like. Ignoring your puppy when he jumps up at you, for example, will help him learn not to bother, but he will learn even more quickly if you also reward him for keeping all four paws on the floor.

A game of consequences

Modern dog training is a game of consequences and it isn't difficult to play. But to stay ahead of the game you need to remember that your puppy is learning all the time, not just when you are intentionally teaching him. Consequences can work against us as well as for us. Great behaviours that you have trained can easily be extinguished. If you persistently forget to reward your puppy for coming when you whistle, he will gradually stop coming. Bad behaviours, such as yapping, can easily be accidentally reinforced by intermittently giving the puppy your attention while he is making a noise. So it is important to remember to save your attention for when he is being quiet. Good behaviours can also easily be unintentionally punished. If you immediately put your puppy on the lead after calling him to you, the recall has effectively been punished, and the puppy will soon stop coming back. Simple strategies, such as playing with your puppy for a few minutes before you clip his lead on, can make the world of difference.

Where possible, it is a great idea to reduce opportunities for your puppy to get into mischief or learn bad habits. Moving the bin into another room to prevent bin-raiding activities, and putting your precious stuff away will save much conflict.

From theory to practice

You know how the game works now. You are aware of how easy it is to punish or reward the wrong behaviours accidentally. You understand why we use a combination of reinforcement and extinction to control and modify a puppy's behaviour. You are almost ready to put all this theory into practice.

The beauty of this elegant system is that it can be applied to absolutely anything your puppy does. It can be used to teach your dog to carry out new behaviours on your command, to fix problem behaviours that have been accidentally created in the past, or simply to have a go at teaching your dog a few tricks. Most of all, the system is fun – for both of you.

As a human being, you have enormous control over the resources available to your puppy. Use it! Save titbits to give him later when he is resting quietly in his basket. Use his food to teach nice manners. Make the things he wants to do, such as playing with other dogs, or even simply going through a door, dependent on the thing *you* want him to do.

It isn't as difficult as it sounds, because once you have got the hang of it, the game of consequences will become second nature. You will soon learn to wait for silence before letting your puppy out of his crate, or to wait for him to sit before you open a door for him to pass through. Making little changes in *your* behaviour to generate changes in *his* will come naturally. And don't worry if your puppy's behaviour isn't perfect right now. Whilst it is always easier to establish good habits if bad habits are avoided, bad habits can often be resolved, as we'll discover in Part Three.

We have spent quite a substantial amount of time looking at how puppies learn new behaviours, and in the chapters that follow you will be able to observe the practical applications of this knowledge – both in creating *learned* behaviours, such as teaching your puppy to toilet outdoors rather than on your carpets, and in reducing some of those annoying instinctive puppy behaviours, such as grabbing and biting at people's hands and feet.

Don't worry if your puppy's behaviour is not perfect yet.

Perhaps, most importantly, this knowledge will help you avoid falling into the trap of inadvertently creating problems in your puppy where no problems existed to begin with. You will be able to avoid having to cope with a whining or fussy puppy that cannot bear to be left alone. You will be able to teach your puppy new and interesting skills and to establish good foundations on which to raise a model canine citizen.

Learning to be friendly

Whilst common behavioural problems may cause conflict between puppies and their new owners, they are rarely a serious threat to society at large. If your dog begs at the table, if he puts his muddy feet on your visitors, digs holes in your lawn, or barks when you get your car keys out, you may be happy to live with that, rather than attempt to resolve it.

Aggression, however, is an altogether more serious matter. The next chapter focuses exclusively on how you can raise a friendly puppy, and help to avoid the disaster that is a dangerous dog.

SUMMARY

We will look more closely at practical training techniques in Part Two, but for now here is a summary of what you need to remember from this chapter.

- Think carefully about the consequences of your puppy's actions.
- Avoid reinforcing bad behaviour, including with your attention.
- Reward good behaviour with lots of attention and desirable treats.
- Don't let great behaviours die.
- Restrict your puppy's access to things you do not want him to touch.

3
Raising a friendly puppy

t is impossible to overestimate the importance of good temperament in a domestic dog. It is without question the most powerful influence in determining whether or not a dog will fit into family life, bring pleasure to his owners, and even whether or not he is likely to be abandoned by the family who once loved him.

In many countries, including the United Kingdom, dogs are widely liked and trusted. Many people willingly approach and even embrace strange dogs without hesitation. The majority of dogs never abuse the trust bestowed upon them, but attacks by dogs are not uncommon and in many, if not most, cases they could have been avoided.

Everyone's friend?

People often assume that, through years of domestication, dogs are naturally predisposed to be friendly towards *all* humans. They assume that the exceptions to this rule have been abused or badly bred. This is not the case. Dogs are instinctively friendly towards their family members, but extending that friendliness towards the *whole* of society is more complicated.

If someone stops to pat your puppy in the street, you will want him to respond in a warm and friendly way – not just while he is small, but even more importantly as he grows up. He needs your help to make this happen, because he is genetically programmed to become wary of strangers at quite an early age. And not without good reason.

For a wild dog living in a dangerous world, friendliness is likely to result in an early demise. Nature's assumption is that something you have never come across before is likely to be dangerous, so you had better regard it with great suspicion. Many wild animals share this natural instinct for self-protection. As a result, *indiscriminate* friendliness is not a characteristic that your dog's ancestors have passed on to him.

So, if indiscriminate friendliness is not a trait passed down from your dog's wolf relatives, where does it come from? Why are most adult dogs friendly?

The window for socialisation

We have seen that wild dogs need to have a natural fear of strange and therefore potentially dangerous creatures, items and events. But dogs are social animals, and nature needs a mechanism to provide puppies with sufficient time to get to know and bond with all the members of their social group, before this fear of novelty kicks in.

In a wolf family, it is vital that each cub learns to recognise, and regard with affection, all those adults on whom his safety depends. Consequently, nature has provided a brief window of opportunity during which cubs are unafraid of new objects and experiences. Dogs have inherited this developmental window and the process of domestication has expanded it a little. During this period, puppies will readily bond with those who show them friendship and take care of them. Once it is ended, a natural wariness, and even fear, of novelty sets in.

This short time is the critical period for socialisation. Most puppies are right in the middle of it at the age when they leave for their new homes, which is why puppies are able to move in with total strangers and settle in relatively easily.

The critical period provides time for the puppy to acquaint himself with various aspects of the environment in which he lives, as well as enabling him to bond with his family. A wild puppy gets to know the wind and the rain, rivers and rocks, and to crawl among the undergrowth and feel at home in his natural world. The domestic puppy needs to do the same, though probably in a more urban context.

Used properly, this window of time during which your puppy will accept all newcomers into his life with equal enthusiasm is your ticket to a friendly puppy. This is when we can introduce a puppy to all manner of experiences and he will accept them readily. By the same token, the puppy that is isolated and shut away from new experiences during this important period is likely to be fearful and suspicious of many aspects of normal life. This can take a great deal of work to overcome and is quite a handicap for the dog concerned.

Most importantly, fear in dogs can have serious consequences.

Triggers for aggression

In most cases, the catalyst for aggression in any dog is fear. Dogs do not normally use aggression to manipulate others. Aggression is triggered when the dog feels vulnerable or threatened.

In the natural world, wild carnivores are often exposed to danger. Aggression in the face of fear is sometimes needed for survival, but a wild dog or wolf has choices. When placed in danger, he can usually choose whether to fight or to run. He makes that choice based on what is of most benefit to him and those that share his genes. He may choose to *fight* to protect the resources he needs in order to survive, access to food for example. He may choose to *run* from predators much larger or heavier than he is in order to avoid death or injury.

A domestic dog, on the other hand, rarely needs to fight for resources, such as food, because we provide those for him. Most of the time, his best option when afraid would therefore be to run. But life is not that simple, and a domestic dog is frequently placed in situations from which he cannot escape.

A nervous dog may be faced on a daily basis with events and experiences that frighten him badly while being completely prevented from separating himself from the source of his fear. Some dogs are afraid of children, some are afraid of men, others of old people, vehicles, cows, things that flap in the wind, or even of being outside. In most cases, this fear is due to a lack of exposure to the source of his fear during the critical window. Unfortunately, if a dog cannot run away from the source of his fear, and is sufficiently afraid, he may well feel that he has no option but to fight.

The purpose of socialisation

Since we know that aggression in dogs is largely based in fear, getting rid of that fear is a top priority. That is the purpose of the process that we call socialisation. A significant factor in creating a fearless puppy is the breadth and extent of the experiences he is exposed to during his fearless phase. Socialising a puppy means deliberately ensuring he is exposed to as many new experiences as possible.

A busy town centre helps accustom this puppy to crowds.

Your puppy will need to meet people of all shapes and sizes, old and young, male and female. He will need to be exposed to cars and lorries, trains and tractors, dogs and cats, and various other sights and sounds of human civilisation. It will be a busy few weeks.

Breed differences

Over many generations of selective breeding, we have bred dogs in all shapes and sizes. Our breeding programmes have also influenced the temperament of our domestic dogs. We have bred some dogs that have a reduced fear of novelty when adult. These are less likely to be suspicious of strangers, even if the socialisation process has been somewhat brief, or less than thorough. You will be aware that some breeds of dog are particularly known for their friendly temperaments. Most of us know a happy-go-lucky Labrador or a bouncy and affectionate Golden Retriever. But there are many exceptions to this rule.

Unfortunately, we have not bred these characteristics into our dogs consistently or accurately enough to rely upon them. Some dogs will be indiscriminately friendly simply through growing up in a normal home environment and getting out and about with the family. Others will have a friendly temperament *only* if extensively and deliberately socialised by their owners. Identifying which dog is which is problematic, and there may be differences between individuals of the *same* breed.

Your puppy needs to meet all kinds of vehicles.

Predicting temperament

Sadly, we simply cannot accurately predict the outcome of a dog's temperament based on his breeding or parentage. How fearful a dog becomes when exposed to novel situations, and the way in which he reacts when afraid, will vary even between members of the same litter. It is *always* a good idea to pick a dog whose parents have a great temperament, from a breed that has a reputation for good temperament, but this is just tipping the balance in your favour. You have no way of knowing how much the good nature of your puppy's parents was influenced by their environment (i.e. by the way in which they were socialised) and how much of it was inherited.

The only way virtually to guarantee an indiscriminately friendly dog is to socialise him thoroughly and effectively. Don't forget, isolating a puppy of any breed during the window for socialisation, *no matter how great their inherited potential for good temperament,* is likely to result in a fearful and potentially aggressive dog.

Your options therefore are limited. You do need to put some effort into deliberately socialising your puppy. And here is the really important point: you need to do it quickly.

Time is short

By the time your puppy is twelve weeks old the window for socialisation is beginning to close and by sixteen weeks it is all but shut. This means you have a relatively short space of time in which to achieve quite a lot.

Hopefully, the socialisation process will have been started by your puppy's breeder, but you cannot rely on this. You will need to be methodical about socialising your puppy thoroughly, starting when you bring him home at eight weeks old and covering the next four weeks of his life. In Part Two you will find information and suggestions for getting this process under way, and to make sure that you cover all the bases.

Whilst we all want our puppy to be friendly to the children and adults that he meets during the course of his daily life, some people also like the idea of a dog that protects their home. Let's have a brief look at how that works.

Guarding your property

You will naturally want your dog to be friendly to your guests. However, you may also hope that when he is grown up, your puppy will guard your home against intruders. In my opinion, achieving this dual objective is very difficult and in attempting to do so you may be treading a dangerous path. To persuade a dog actually to guard your property, he needs to be *afraid* of anyone who invades what he considers to be *his territory*. Guard dogs are incapable of being selective. The toddler who slips through your hedge looking for his ball will be treated in the same way as your midnight burglar. It really is not worth the risk.

Some perfectly friendly dogs will bark when your home is approached, or when someone knocks on the door. However, many friendly and well-social-ised dogs bark very rarely. Teaching or encouraging dogs to bark can cause more problems than it solves, because barking can easily escalate and become

You have a relatively short time in which to achieve quite a lot.

a nuisance. I talk to many people who cannot stop their dogs from barking. Constant barking can be very stressful to live with, and can even impact on a dog's chances of staying with his family in the long term.

Raising a quiet and friendly dog is simply too important a priority to risk jeopardising with attempts to raise a guard dog, too.

Your responsibility

Socialising our puppies is vital, and your commitment to this will help to ensure that your puppy grows up confident and friendly. The effects of socialisation are a bit like compound interest on your savings. The more you put in, the more you get out. The more experiences your puppy learns to accept, the more easily he accepts each new experience. The object is to end up with a dog that is able to cope happily with almost any eventuality. I say almost because there are always exceptions. We need to be aware of our dog's limitations and protect him from being put in situations where he may feel very threatened.

Any dog, no matter how well socialised, is likely to become afraid when he is injured, for example, or when faced with an experience he simply cannot match against any of his experiences so far. If your dog is hurt, you need to assume he may bite. If your dog is exposed to human behaviour he does not understand, and is not allowed to move away, you need to be willing to entertain the possibility that he may react with aggression. Even if he has been well socialised with children, you cannot guarantee that your dog has been exposed to all the sorts of noises that children sometimes make, especially a child that is very scared, or upset. We cannot prepare a dog for every possibility. Toddlers, for example, with their lack of empathy, may sometimes hit dogs, or simply cuddle them too tightly. For this reason, it is vital that dogs are always supervised around small children.

A most important task

A fully socialised dog has come across all manner of people, objects, vehicles, animals and buildings, and is not afraid of anything he meets on a daily basis. Essentially, the whole human race and all its comings and goings has become part of his accepted social group. Socialising your new puppy thoroughly may be the single most important thing you ever do for him. It takes a little commitment, but it is worth every moment you spend on the process.

Your puppy needs your help to grow up friendly.

Understanding the relevance and importance of effective socialisation will help you cope with its sometimes inconvenient demands. In some respects, the process gets easier as your puppy grows, if only because you don't have to carry him everywhere once his vaccinations are complete.

In the coming months your puppy will change a good deal. He will grow in confidence as he matures and as you teach him that the world holds nothing to fear. Some dramatic changes will occur in his physical strength and size. Understanding how your puppy changes as he matures will help you know what to expect of him and will help you to nurture him within the limits of his capabilities. Let's move on to the next chapter, and find out how your puppy will develop over the next few weeks.

 SUMMARY
- Puppies need our help to become sociable.
- Expose your puppy to as many people, sights and sounds as possible before he is twelve weeks old.
- Speed is of the essence in socialising your puppy.
- Don't plan to train him to be a guard dog or to bark.

4
Influencing growth and development

Puppies grow up very fast and the cuddly bundle in your arms today will look very different in a few months' time. In the space of a single year most puppies complete the bulk of their physical growth and have become sexually mature – rapid growth and development are fairly important in a social predator whose parents would normally reproduce on an annual basis.

Domestication has had an effect on the development of our dogs, though. Unlike wolves, dogs retain some juvenile behavioural characteristics, a willingness to play for example, for most of their lives. Whilst most puppies are not mentally mature at a year old, and some larger dogs still have some growing to do, a year is approximately what it takes to turn your tiny puppy into a full-sized

In a few months' time this cuddly puppy will look very different.

adult dog. And a year, more or less, is not a very long time in which to grow up and find your place in the modern world.

People tend to worry quite a bit about growth – how much their puppy should weigh, and how tall he should be, at any given age. It is tempting to make comparisons with other dogs, but there is great variety of form, even in dogs of the same breed. In this chapter we'll look at the growth and development process, and how you can influence it in your puppy's best interests.

I'll also be talking about ways in which you can make the most of the opportunities that the different stages in his development will offer you.

It is not just your puppy's body that will be changing rapidly during this time; his mind will be maturing, too. For the first few weeks in his new home, a puppy is emotionally dependent on his carers; he won't want to stray far from the trusted grown-ups that represent his security and safety. This dependency can be a great asset.

The dependent phase

This brief stage in your puppy's life is marked by his need to be close to you. It includes the all-important window for socialisation, which we looked at in the previous chapter. Your role during this phase is to make your puppy feel safe and secure in our human world, to teach him to be friendly, and to make the most of the opportunities that your puppy's dependence offers you. In particular, this is an opportunity to establish a great recall response, and a close bond with your puppy.

The dependent puppy is afraid of losing contact with his grown-ups, so you can place him on the ground just about anywhere, set off in one direction, and he will trot along after you. The faster you move, the more he will want to stay with you, and the more times you change direction, the more he will concentrate on what you are doing. His primary goal is to make sure that the contact between you is not broken. This lovely inherited behaviour was essential in wild dogs, where separation from the family could have tragic consequences for a puppy.

Sadly, many new puppy owners are not aware of this wonderful following instinct that all young puppies possess. Afraid of losing their precious pups, they keep them securely on a lead throughout this period, missing out on the time that their puppy should be spending learning to follow them. They then take the plunge and let the puppy off the lead to give him his freedom for the very first time as he enters 'emerging independence'. This can be disastrous, because the

A tiny puppy will follow you everywhere you go.

puppy that is becoming independent may have little sense of danger, and no fear of getting lost.

During the early part of the dependent phase, your puppy is physically quite vulnerable. He tends to cling around your feet and is often small enough to trip over. He investigates everything he finds with his mouth and is open to injury and poisoning if not properly supervised. His immune system is not fully developed and his digestive system is prone to the occasional upset. If he gets sick, he may become dehydrated quite quickly, and if he seems unwell, you should not delay seeking veterinary help.

Just as we do with toddlers, it is easier to care for the dependent puppy if you make a few changes to your home and garden before he arrives. We'll look at those in the final chapter of this first part of the book.

Emerging independence

The next phase in your puppy's life, emerging independence, is heralded by a fairly rapid increase in confidence and an equally rapid decrease in your puppy's dependence on your presence to feel safe. The age at which this phase begins varies from breed to breed and from individual to individual.

Many dogs will reach emerging independence in the final third of their first year. A few will reach this point much earlier, and a very few will remain highly dependent for the rest of their lives. You need to assume, however, that the independent phase could begin at any point after four months. As the puppy grows in confidence, he will start to take pleasure in exploring by himself and in moving farther away from you.

As emerging independence gets under way, your dog will leave behind some of the more annoying puppy behaviours. Teething is usually over by around seven months and your puppy will no longer be biting everything in sight. His need to chew the furniture may start to subside, and he should be reliably clean in the house, provided that you don't leave him shut in for too long.

However, emerging independence brings its own challenges, and this is the point at which many people get into difficulties with training their puppies. In Part Two, to ensure this doesn't happen to you, I'll explain how you can establish the foundations of good behaviour and take your first steps in training your puppy to be obedient.

Physical growth

The rapid growth that takes place during your puppy's first six months needs to be fuelled with adequate quantities of appropriate food. Too much food and the puppy may grow too quickly or become too fat. Too little food, or food of the wrong kind, and the puppy may not have sufficient nutrients to keep him strong and healthy. The object is to provide sufficient nutrients for steady, sustained growth, and no more.

Most people worry that their puppy might not be getting enough to eat. In reality, it is unusual for a puppy in a caring home to lack sufficient nutrients for growth. Overfeeding is far more common.

Weight control

Perhaps one of the greatest threats to your dog's health in our modern age is excessive weight gain. Obesity is a growing and serious problem in domestic dogs. Overfeeding a small puppy may lead to more rapid growth, which in turn is believed to be a contributory factor in serious joint problems, including hip dysplasia. As people have grown larger, so have their dogs, and the sad truth is that many dogs are now overweight. With obesity comes a raft of other problems, including diabetes and heart troubles. It seems we are creating a mirror image of our own medical problems for our four-legged friends.

It is really important to keep your puppy slim.

Temptations for people to overeat are many, and the psychological and emotional aspects of human obesity are complex, but the situation for dogs is far simpler. Your puppy cannot open a tin or a packet, nor pop into his local shop. He cannot ever decide what or when to eat. Only you can do that for him. You have complete control over how fat he becomes, and one of the most important things you will ever do for his health is to keep him slim.

Obviously, in order to maintain your dog at a healthy weight, there needs to be a good balance between food intake and exercise. It takes a great deal of exercise to burn off a few extra calories, and small puppies have very different exercise needs from adult dogs, as we shall see. So, increasing exercise is not, and never will be, a neat and complete solution to avoiding obesity in puppies. The answer lies first and foremost in controlling how much they eat.

What does 'slim' look like?

People often ask, 'How much should my puppy weigh at ten weeks?' or 'twelve weeks?' This really is not something that anyone can accurately predict. It depends on the genetically predetermined potential size of your puppy as an adult, as well as on how he is fed and cared for. Even puppies in the same litter may vary quite considerably in how much they measure and weigh as adults.

It's all very well knowing that your dog should be slim, but how do you know when he is the right weight? What does 'slim' look like?

Viewed from above, and from the side, your puppy should have a waist. This becomes more pronounced as he grows. If you can feel the knobbles along his spine without pressing very hard, he is too thin. And you should not be able to see or feel his hips. His rump should feel firm and smooth. Initially, you should not be able to see your puppy's ribs, although if you run your hands firmly along his sides and can just feel them, that's fine. Once your puppy is over five months old or so, you may find he gets very gangly for a while and you may be able to see the last two or three ribs, especially when he twists or turns, or eats and drinks. In some breeds, often those built for speed such as greyhounds or whippets, a couple of visible ribs is normal at all times.

If you think your puppy is getting a little too thin, then by all means increase his rations. But don't go mad! If you are unsure whether or not your puppy is a healthy weight, don't hesitate to take him along to your vet, who will be able to put your mind at rest, and advise you on any changes you may need to make to his diet.

We mentioned earlier that keeping your puppy slim as he grows will help to protect his developing joints. Being the correct weight is one factor you can control, but it is not the only one. Avoiding excessive exercise is another.

The five-minute rule

'When can I take my puppy for a walk?' is something I am asked a great deal. It is not unusual to find people taking tiny twelve-week-old pups for quite long walks on a lead. However, a puppy's bones are still soft and growing, and it is believed that inappropriate exercise may damage the growth plates within them. This damage might then cause or exacerbate joint problems later in life, especially if the puppy has been unfortunate enough to inherit a tendency to hip dysplasia.

Consequently, experts often recommend that puppies be walked for no more than five minutes per day for each month of their age, starting when they are around four months old. This means no more than twenty minutes of exercise per day for a four-month-old puppy or thirty minutes at six months.

I should make it clear that there are no official studies to back up this rule, although it is certainly widely acknowledged to be a sensible precaution. One recent Norwegian study suggests that it may be the type of exercise rather than the quantity that is most relevant. Of all the puppies studied, the ones most likely to develop joint problems were those that had been allowed access to steps before three months of age. It makes sense, therefore, to carry small puppies up and down steep steps or in and out of vehicles, and to avoid teaching or encouraging dogs to jump much before their first birthday.

Your influence

The final size reached by your dog will depend on a combination of factors, including his genes, whether or not he is neutered, and his general health and diet. Dogs of very large breeds may take two years or more to reach their adult size. A sick or chronically underfed puppy may never reach the size that nature intended; a chronically overfed puppy may exceed it.

Providing a puppy with the right amount of food, and making sure he grows and develops at a healthy rate need not be complicated. You don't need to keep weighing your puppy any more than you would keep weighing your children. Just keep an eye on his appearance, and make sure he does not get too thin or too fat. Unlike our children, we are not preparing our dogs for life in the world without us, and it is important that our dogs do not become *too* independent. So remember to use your small puppy's dependent phase to build a habit of

The five-minute rule does not include gentle play in the garden.

Larger breed puppies may take two years to reach their final size.

following you around whenever you are outdoors together. This will stand you in good stead when it comes to future training exercises.

Knowing how to keep your puppy's growth on track may be straightforward enough, but deciding what exactly to feed him may be another matter. There are some very different approaches to feeding puppies and adult dogs, and many new puppy owners find the choices available to them bewildering. In the next chapter, we are going to explore the often contentious topic of how and what to feed your puppy.

 SUMMARY

- Use your puppy's initial dependency to establish a close bond.
- Allow your puppy to follow you off the lead to lay the foundation of a good recall response.
- Avoid overfeeding your puppy.
- Don't expect him to walk long distances.
- Carry him up steps and discourage jumping to protect his bones and joints.

5

Feeding your puppy

We are all very aware that long-term health is at least partly dependent on a decent diet, and that this applies to our dogs as much as it applies to us. What constitutes a good diet for a dog is, however, a subject that is often hotly debated. This chapter looks at the options that are available to you for feeding your puppy, and investigates the pros and cons of each.

For thousands of years, dogs were probably fed on the scraps left over by their human companions. But, as the status of dogs has risen, and as people have acquired more disposable income, an entire industry has developed around the production and distribution of commercially prepared dog food.

The rise and rise of kibble

Kibble is the dried and pelleted dog food that you can buy in packets and sacks from pet shops and online. It is a relatively recent invention, yet within a few years of its arrival, many of the UK's dog owners were happy converts. Kibble was a much more convenient way to feed our dogs. No more struggling with can openers and sharp tin lids, or thawing out blocks of smelly whale meat. No more staggering back to the car with half a hundredweight of canned dog food in your shopping trolley each week, and no more worrying about how much dog biscuit to mix with the contents of each tin. The vast majority of dogs in the UK are now fed on kibble, and for a long time very few people questioned whether or not this was a good thing.

More recently, the effect that this shift away from wet food and onto dried food has had on canine health (if any) has become the subject of intense speculation. It is not possible to own a dog for very long without coming across the raw versus kibble debate.

Growth of interest in raw feeding

Over the last few years or so, there has been a steady growth in enthusiasm for feeding dogs on a more natural diet based on raw meat and bones. You may have heard it referred to as the BARF diet (Biologically Appropriate Raw Food), or RMB (Raw Meaty Bones) diet. These are actually two slightly different approaches to raw feeding.

Many thousands of dogs in the UK and abroad are now fed on a diet of raw meat and bones, or in the case of BARF, raw meat, bones and vegetables. One of the most widely reported benefits of raw feeding is improved dental health. This is significant because, according to the Royal Veterinary College, 87 per cent of dogs aged over three years in the UK currently suffer from periodontal disease. This shocking statistic has wider implications than it might for you and me, because dogs often require a general anaesthetic for even quite basic dental treatment.

The return to raw feeding is supported and indeed promoted by a number of veterinary surgeons, including Tom Lonsdale (RMB) and Ian Billingshurst

Some people choose to feed their dogs a raw diet.

(BARF), both of whom have written books on the subject. But it must be said that probably the *majority* of veterinary professionals do not currently support raw feeding and many are decidedly against it. Those opposed to feeding raw meat and bones have a number of concerns, including the following:

- Bones might cause gastrointestinal blockage.
- Splintered bones could penetrate the digestive tract.
- Dogs might catch parasites from raw meat.
- Raw feeding might lead to serious infections.
- Bones might cause choking.
- It might be too difficult to provide a balanced diet.
- Bones might cause broken teeth.

Some of this sounds plausible enough, and pretty scary. But what, statistically, are the risks?

Unfortunately, we still don't have any reliable data linking any of the above with any particular diet, one way or the other. It is true that vets do sometimes see dogs with severe constipation and impacted bone in their digestive tract, but it is not clear whether these dogs have been fed recreational bones, cooked bones, or raw bones well wrapped in meat; nor do we know if these bones have been fed to dogs that are used to digesting bone on a regular basis; nor do we have any idea what proportion of completely raw-fed dogs (if any) get into difficulties in this way.

The situation with regard to infections is the same. At the time of writing, there are no long-term studies comparing the incidence of salmonella, for example, or any other food-borne disease, in raw-fed dogs with the incidence in kibble-fed dogs. We do know that salmonella occurs in raw chicken, and it has been found in kibble, too. What we also know is that most healthy dogs seem to be able to consume all manner of unpleasant substances, including the faeces of other animals, without becoming ill. And most raw-fed dogs consume large quantities of raw chicken without contracting salmonella or any other unpleasant illness that would almost certainly strike down you or me if we attempted to do the same. In fact, the risk of you infecting yourself through *handling* the contaminated meat is probably far greater than any risk to your dog.

Some of the potential hazards of raw feeding can probably be avoided or reduced by taking sensible precautions. Feeding large weight-bearing bones, for example, is more likely to damage your dog's teeth than smaller bones, such as ribs.

Your dog's digestive system

Those opposed to raw feeding will tell you that 'modern dogs are not wolves'. They argue that dogs have evolved extensively since they became domesticated many thousands of years ago and adapted to life as scavengers, and are no longer suited to eating raw meat and bone. It is only fair to point out that, in evolutionary terms, ten or even twenty thousand years is actually not very long. When compared, the digestive tracts of dogs and wolves are, in fact, very similar. Both have jaws designed for tearing meat and crushing bone and the very short digestive tracts typical of carnivores. Both are capable of ingesting and digesting meat, bones and skin on a regular day-to-day basis.

The consequences of feeding kibble

The proponents of raw feeding will often declare that kibble is harmful, and responsible for all kinds of health problems, such as allergies and digestive troubles. But the truth is that there is no evidence to support many of these claims. As far as we know most dogs will thrive and live long and happy lives on kibble.

Kibble-fed dogs tend to produce larger quantities of softer and smellier faeces than raw-fed dogs. Dogs that have soft stools may need their anal glands

Modern dogs are not wolves but share a similar skeleton and digestive system.

emptying. This usually involves a visit to the vet (you can be taught to do it your-self, but it is an unpleasant and smelly process). Raw-fed dogs that get sufficient bone in their diet do not need their anal glands emptying because their stools are firm.

There is, however, an altogether more serious problem that may be associated with certain types of kibble. You may know that bloat is a condition that involves a serious swelling of the stomach. In dogs, this gastric dilation or swelling may be accompanied by a rotation or twisting of the stomach. This rotation cuts off the blood supply at either end of the stomach and results in the rapid decline and death of the dog if not treated very quickly. Vets call this condition GDV (gastric dilation and volvulus) and it is a particular problem in some large, deep-chested breeds of dog. A study carried out at Purdue University, Indiana, USA, showed that GDV is more common in dogs fed kibble with a high fat content or a high citric-acid content. A more recent study from Pennsylvania published in 2012 listed dry food generally as a risk factor. Bloat is also more common in dogs that are related to bloat sufferers or that have suffered from bloat in the past.

Interestingly, there have been a number of cases of salmonella acquired through contact with kibble and there have been a significant number of recalls of kibble during the last few years due to contamination.

Which is safer?

As you can see, just like raw feeding, kibble probably has its risks, especially for certain types of dog. Without properly controlled studies it is not really possible to determine which is the safer *long-term* option for our dogs. Studies on dog food are normally sponsored by dog-food manufacturers and it is not in their interests to pay for studies that might reduce the sales of their products. So we are likely to remain in ignorance for the time being.

Bearing in mind that good evidence in support of there being a right and a wrong way to feed your dog is sadly lacking, you'll need to make your choice based on your personal circumstances and concerns.

Reasons to feed kibble

Feeding kibble is very convenient. You simply open a packet and pour it out. Kibble is also perfectly balanced with all the nutrients that your dog requires. Feeding a rapidly growing and developing puppy is not the same as feeding an adult dog. Getting the nutrient balance right is particularly important for puppies because their diet must accommodate their growth and development.

Although I feed my own dogs on an entirely raw diet, including puppies, I do counsel *some caution* before encouraging others to do the same.

The following are, I believe, good reasons to consider feeding kibble:

- You are bringing home a kibble-raised puppy.
- You have no previous experience of raw feeding.
- You have children under ten years old.
- You do not have a reliable source of cheap meaty bones.
- You do not have adequate space to dedicate to meat preparation.
- You do not have a large freezer.
- You dislike handling raw meat.
- You are very worried about the potential risks of raw feeding.
- You intend to travel a great deal with your dog.

Let's have a look at some of these in a bit more detail.

Tummy troubles Puppies are prone to stomach upsets. These upsets can be triggered by a change in environment, and especially by a change in diet. If your breeder has raised your puppy on kibble for the last few weeks, think very hard before tampering with the status quo. House-training presents sufficient challenges on its own, without adding to them.

Previous experience If this is your first puppy, you will be on quite a steep learning curve. Do you really want to take on a whole new project?

Young children You also need to consider that raw-fed dogs make a mess. They hold down their food with their paws, and pull and tear at it with their mouths. Raw meat and meat juices get caught in the fur on their legs, faces and (in some breeds) ears. Children are very unreliable at washing their hands. Your four-year-old will also at some point let your puppy lick her face, no matter how hard you try to avoid it. I personally feel that a dog covered in raw chicken juice is not an ideal playmate for a child.

Resources Raw feeding takes up a lot of space. Unless you want to visit a butcher on a daily basis you will need to have the food delivered in bulk, and that means frozen. You will need plenty of freezer space to store the food, and fridge space to defrost it. You will also need to be knowledgeable about handling and preparing raw meat safely, and be comfortable with doing so.

It is worth bearing in mind that we use food extensively in training puppies and in helping them to make good associations with different aspects of their lives. This is simpler to do if you can easily divide up their meals and use them as rewards. The kibble-fed puppy's food can all be used in this way to help him settle into his new life. This can also be done with raw food, but it is a messy business!

Reasons to feed raw

Feeding raw is not as straightforward as feeding kibble, but provides dogs with a great deal of pleasure. Improvements in dental health and the resolution of anal-gland problems in dogs switched from kibble to a raw diet are widely reported. A raw diet may confer other health benefits but we have no firm evidence for those at the moment. Some of the claims made for raw food, shiny coats for example, are also reported by dog owners feeding good-quality kibbles. There are, however, some other factors that might make feeding your puppy on a raw diet a good choice for your family.

- **Your puppy has been raised from birth on raw food.**
- **You have other raw-fed dogs.**
- **You have access to large quantities of meaty bones.**
- **You have a large, deep-chested breed of dog, or your puppy has a close relative that has suffered from bloat.**

Your choice will really depend on how you feel about these very different ways of feeding, and on your own family situation and lifestyle.

Use part of your puppy's daily rations as training aids.

Other options

Kibble or raw are not the only options. You can still purchase traditional wet dog foods in cans or trays, and many owners prepare their dog's food themselves by mixing some raw meat in with home-cooked food and perhaps some kibble. None of these methods is right or wrong, although you may find it difficult to get appropriate advice and support if you feed your dog in an unusual way or on a changing diet. If you are preparing home-made food for your dog, or feeding household scraps, it is very important to bear in mind that dogs are primarily carnivores and need a substantial proportion of their food in the form of protein and fat, rather than as carbohydrates, such as potatoes, rice or pasta. It is also important to be aware that a number of human foods are toxic to dogs if fed in sufficient quantities. These include common items, such as grapes, raisins and onions. Xylitol, a sweetener found in chewing gum, is particularly dangerous. You will meet people who tell you their dog eats chocolate without ill effects but chocolate can and does kill dogs, as every vet will confirm. Easter and Christmas are particular high-risk periods for accidental poisoning. Dogs do not need cakes, pastries and confectionery, and feeding them to your puppy may wreck his teeth and possibly his health, so don't be tempted to indulge him.

Puppies don't need milk

One common mistake that new puppy owners make is in providing their puppies with milk. Eight-week-old puppies are completely weaned and don't need milk in any shape or form. You can buy substitute bitch's milk from large pet shops, and some older breeders still raise puppies on two milk feeds and two meat feeds a day, but we now know that this is neither necessary nor beneficial. Cow's milk is particularly inappropriate and may cause diarrhoea. All your puppy needs to eat is *either* a balanced diet of raw meats and bone, *or* a complete commercial puppy kibble.

Making your choice

The whole raw-feeding controversy has some similarities with the human breast-feeding debate. Raw feeders can be quite evangelical in their claims about the benefits of raw feeding. People who decide not to feed raw can be left feeling quite inadequate and wondering if their dog will die of some horrible disease in the future as a result.

You need to make the choice based on what feels right for your family, but personally I feel that many new puppy owners will be happier and more confident feeding their puppies on a good-quality kibble. Kibble-fed puppies will benefit from regular tooth brushing, and studies have shown that your efforts in this respect will help to protect your dog from gum disease.

Puppies thrive on kibble too.

Feeding schedules

Whatever diet you choose to feed your puppy, he will need it to be divided up into several small meals. He needs so much to eat at this point in his life that he cannot digest it all in one go. Small puppies need at least four meals a day until they are around three months old. Each meal should amount to one quarter of his daily food allowance.

If you are feeding kibble, the manufacturer will give you guidelines about the recommended daily quantity required. This tends to be more with cheaper kibbles as they contain more fillers. Many puppies will eat far more than one quarter of their daily ration at one sitting, but be aware that if you try to feed fewer, larger meals too soon, your puppy will get diarrhoea. Quite aside from the unpleasantness of this outcome, diarrhoea in puppies can be serious, and sometimes can be hard to resolve.

By three months of age, many puppies can cope with their daily ration being divided into three larger meals a day. If the new regime upsets his tummy, go back to four meals a day for a week or two, then try again. At six months you can usually drop down to two meals a day, and many raw-fed dogs will do well on just one meal a day from around a year old.

Your healthy puppy

There is plenty of information in this chapter for you to consider and if, like most new puppy owners, you decide to feed your puppy on kibble, you will probably have the support and approval of your vet. If you decide to go the raw route, please read Chapter 25, 'Switching to raw feeding', in Part Three of this book. This chapter will help you make a smooth transition to raw feeding, reduce any risks and avoid some common mistakes.

Of course, there is more to a happy puppy than plenty of nutritious food. Your puppy will also depend on you to keep him safe from disease and free from parasites. Healthcare is the topic of our next chapter. We'll be looking at what you need to do in the way of providing veterinary care and attention for your young dog, and at basic healthcare strategies that you can implement at home.

SUMMARY

- Weigh up the pros and cons of feeding kibble or raw food.
- Be aware of bloat.
- Don't allow him milk or chocolate – or any other sweets, cakes or pastries.
- Until he's three months old, divide your puppy's daily ration into at least four meals.

6

Healthcare

odern medicines and programmes of vaccination have made puppy-hood, like childhood, a much safer stage in life. Not so very long ago, puppyhood was a risky time. Dogs could catch a number of horrible diseases, which were often fatal, particularly for puppies. However, not everyone agrees that vaccinations are now the best way to protect our puppies from ill health. So in this chapter, we look at the options available to you and at the current evidence relating to their safety and efficacy. We will also look at how to keep your puppy free from parasites and at how to judge whether or not your puppy is sick and in need of veterinary attention.

A healthy puppy is full of energy.

The healthy puppy

A healthy puppy is full of energy when he wakes from a nap. He plays enthusiastically and looks bright and bouncy. He sleeps often, deeply and quietly, although he may twitch his paws and make little sounds when he is dreaming. Many new puppies will get mildly upset tummies with the stress of moving home, and for the first few days some puppies will be carsick each time you take them out. This is normal.

Since puppies are so small, they can go downhill rather fast if they get sick. So it is important to contact your vet if an upset tummy does not clear up quickly, or if you have any concerns at all.

The following are reasons to call your vet without delay:

- If your puppy seems listless or won't eat.
- If he has persistent diarrhoea, or is sick more than once within forty-eight hours, or twice in a week.
- If your puppy swallows anything you think may harm him, cries for no apparent reason or in an unusual way.
- If your puppy's breathing is noisy or laboured.
- If he drags one of his limbs, is unsteady on his feet, or seems to be limping.
- If your puppy has a discharge from any part of his body.
- If your puppy cuts himself, falls badly, or just seems generally off colour.

If you are in any doubt about any aspect of your puppy's health or behaviour, call your vet. He won't think you are making a fuss and would rather see a healthy puppy than risk not seeing a sick one.

There are a number of routine healthcare procedures that your vet will recommend you carry out at regular intervals for your puppy. These include treating him for internal and external parasites, and protecting him from serious diseases with a course of vaccinations.

Many people will be happy to have their puppy vaccinated at his very first veterinary appointment, but increasingly I am coming across people who are concerned about the risks of vaccination in general, or of over-vaccination in particular. I think it is important that these risks are addressed and not dismissed out of hand. So we will be looking at how vaccinations work, and how safe they are, before we move on to some of the other routine healthcare procedures that you will need to consider.

How vaccinations work

Your puppy's body has the ability to detect foreign and therefore potentially dangerous substances. Just like you, your puppy is able to produce antibodies, which identify and neutralise foreign invaders, such as bacteria or viruses. His system is able to recognise germs as dangerous, and so can manufacture the anti-bodies that he needs to protect himself. However, this manufacturing process takes time, and if a disease is serious enough, the puppy may not be able to manufacture sufficient antibodies in time to save his life.

What vaccination does, effectively, is provide the body with a memory of the necessary antibodies in advance. So if and when your puppy is exposed to the disease that he has been vaccinated against, his body is ready and prepared to fight it successfully.

What are we vaccinating against?

The vaccination programme recommended by your veterinary surgeon will protect your puppy from a number of serious diseases, and these recommendations may change over time.

At the time of writing, in the UK, the RSPCA recommends that all dogs are routinely vaccinated against the following diseases, but for the most up-to-date information, always check with your vet.

- Canine parvovirus
- Canine distemper
- Leptospirosis
- Infectious Canine Hepatitis

These diseases can all kill your puppy if he comes into contact with them in an unvaccinated state. Many vets will also recommend a vaccination against kennel cough, which is a bit like a canine version of the flu. It's certainly unpleasant but does not usually do any permanent harm to healthy adult dogs, although it can be serious in any dog whose immunity is compromised, such as elderly dogs or those that are already suffering from a serious illness.

Are vaccinations safe?

The Veterinary Medicines Directorate (an agency of the Department for Environment, Food and Rural Affairs – DEFRA) regulates all veterinary medicines in the UK, including vaccines. Before any vaccine can be sold in the UK it must pass a strict, independent, scientific assessment. However, the tests that are carried out do not tell you whether or not the vaccine is safe for *your* dog. They can only tell you that the vaccine is safe for *most* of the dogs that are vaccinated.

There is no doubt that vaccinations can cause side effects. In fact, anything that has an effect is likely to have side effects to *some degree*. Scientists look for treatments that have the minimum of side effects with the maximum of desired effect. One of the difficulties in developing such treatments is that no two puppies will react in exactly the same way. You will get a spectrum of reactions that vary from no apparent side effects at all, right up to serious effects at the other end of the scale. The vast majority of dogs fall in the middle with mild or undetectable side effects.

In 2004, the Animal Health Trust funded a study of over 4,000 dogs. This study found that there was no association between vaccination and illness, such as might be expected due to side effects. In fact, a dog was just as likely to have become ill during the other nine months of the year as it was during the post-vaccination period.

Another study found that when side effects do occur, they are more likely to occur in very small dogs over a year old, and when several vaccinations are given at one time. If you have a small-breed puppy, you might want to talk to your vet about spreading out his vaccinations when you take him for his first annual booster.

For up-to-date information on vaccines, talk to your vet.

Despite the relative safety of modern vaccinations, it is natural to worry about their effect on your puppy. What if *your* puppy is the one who suffers from side effects? People naturally want to know whether there are safer alternatives to conventional veterinary vaccinations.

What about alternatives?

It would be truly amazing if we could find an equally effective and absolutely safe alternative to vaccination, and no doubt many companies would be clamouring to produce it. Sadly, at the moment, all the evidence points to the fact that there is no effective alternative available to us.

You may hear of nosodes – homeopathic preparations – being recommended as an alternative to vaccination. Unfortunately, studies have shown that homeopathic nosodes do not offer any protection against parvovirus and other diseases.

But my friend's dog is fine

The chances are that you will know one or two people who do not have their dogs vaccinated, or who swear by some alternative treatment. So why is it that *their* dogs are in robust health? The answer to that question is a phenomenon called 'herd immunity'.

In any population, as the proportion of individuals that are vaccinated reaches a certain level, the risk to unvaccinated individuals will fall. This is because the unvaccinated individual is less likely to come into contact with the disease. This is what we call herd immunity. However, once the uptake of vaccination in the dog population falls below a critical level, the diseases it protects against begin to increase, and risks to unvaccinated dogs rise sharply.

Relying on herd immunity to keep your dog safe is a risky strategy, because it is not possible to know what the vaccination uptake is like in your area at any given time. Outbreaks of all the canine diseases we vaccinate against still occur throughout the dog population. They have not been completely eradicated, and there is no way to predict when or where the next outbreak will occur.

Do vaccinations wear off?

The effects of vaccination do wear off over time, and your dog will need boosters at intervals. How frequent those intervals should be is a matter of some controversy. At one time annual vaccination was the norm, but there is no doubt that immunity for some of the diseases that we vaccinate dogs against lasts for more than a year. In theory, this means that if a dog is vaccinated against every disease every year, he is receiving more vaccine than he needs, and some dog owners are concerned about the potential effects of over-vaccination.

Vets are now responding to public demand and many are offering variable vaccine schedules. Vaccines vary in the length of time over which they confer immunity. This means that your dog might receive less, or different, vaccines when you take him for his annual booster than he did the previous year. Unfortunately, there is no really precise way of knowing if your dog is still protected against a particular disease without carrying out a blood test. This option is open to you. You can ask your vet to take a sample of blood from your dog and send this off for analysis. Depending on the result of this 'titre' test, you can then choose to have the dog vaccinated only against diseases for which he has no (or low) immunity. It must be said that this is not a cheap option, and still involves sticking a needle into your dog, which he may not be too happy about. But some dog owners feel it is worth it for the peace of mind.

Protecting your new puppy from infection

One of the major concerns that all new puppy owners face is over the safety of their puppy until his course of vaccinations is complete. Your puppy has some protection against diseases even before he is vaccinated, in the form of antibodies passed on from his mother. These antibodies can interfere with the vaccination itself and this is why we need to wait until your puppy is around eight weeks old before he has his first vaccination.

In addition, vets will often counsel the puppy owner not to take the puppy out in public until a week after the final vaccination. As the second vaccination is given three to four weeks after the first, if you follow your vet's instructions to the letter, you could end up with a puppy that has not been out in public until he is twelve or thirteen weeks old.

So how do you reconcile this situation with the urgent need to socialise your puppy? Most people compromise by taking the puppy out and about right from the start, ensuring that they keep him off the ground and away from any direct contact with unvaccinated dogs. This is the strategy I use with my own dogs. It can be difficult with large-breed puppies – carrying a heavy puppy in your arms can be tiring. You may need some kind of bag or sling to carry him in for the last couple of weeks.

Safety at home

If you have a large garden at home, especially one that is frequented by foxes and other wildlife, you may be worried about your puppy catching an infection at home. This is a perfectly natural concern, and indeed some people keep the puppy indoors until his vaccination cover is complete.

The disease that most dog owners are concerned about is canine parvovirus, which is often fatal in puppies. We know that foxes are susceptible to this disease and that the virus can survive for some time in infected faeces. The possibility exists, therefore, *however remote*, that your puppy could be contaminated by contact with fox poo. For this reason, neither I nor anyone else can give you a *guarantee* that he will be safe in your garden.

It is important to keep this in perspective. Most foxes are in good health, and tend not to go wandering around in public when they get sick. Foxes can be discouraged by never leaving out edible items, including bird food, and ensuring that you dispose of food waste in fox-proof bins. It also makes sense to pick up any fox mess left in your garden.

The fact is, keeping your puppy indoors for the next four weeks is potentially harmful. A puppy raised in a sheltered indoor environment is quite likely to be

Puppies need to spend time outdoors.

fearful when exposed to the big wide world at thirteen weeks old. House-training will be delayed and your puppy will have missed out on the simple pleasures of being outdoors.

It isn't an easy decision to make because you will feel overwhelmed by the responsibility of keeping this little dog safe. But if you do decide, as most of us do, to give your puppy access to the garden, try not to worry about him. All across the UK puppies are playing outdoors, and parvovirus in a vaccinated puppy is a very rare occurrence.

Making your decision

As you have no doubt deduced, I am in favour of vaccination for my puppies! But only you can decide where *your* priorities lie. Few people would contest the sense in vaccinating a new puppy. With repeat vaccinations for older dogs, however, there is a wider range of opinion and options.

Do talk to your vet about your concerns. Most vets have dogs themselves and will understand what you are going through. Bear in mind that if you fail to have your puppy vaccinated, in some cases your veterinary insurance will be invalidated and most boarding kennels will not take unvaccinated dogs. Give some thought to the subject of herd immunity because this is what offers good protection to your puppy before his own vaccinations are effective. By vaccinating your dog on a regular basis you will be helping to keep herd immunity at a safe level and protecting the next generation of puppies to come.

Parasites – worms

By the time you bring your puppy home he should have been wormed several times already by his breeder. You may have heard that humans can catch roundworms from puppies and this is true. It is therefore important to worm your puppy regularly and take a few sensible hygiene precautions. Make sure you don't allow the puppy to lick anyone's mouth and that small children wash their hands after playing with him. You should also keep little children well away from anywhere that the puppy has used as a toilet.

Tapeworm infections are also common in dogs, and as he gets older, your puppy will need to be treated regularly to keep him free from these. You can buy worming medicines for older puppies that treat these two types of worm in a single dose. In some parts of the country, lungworms are also an issue. They are

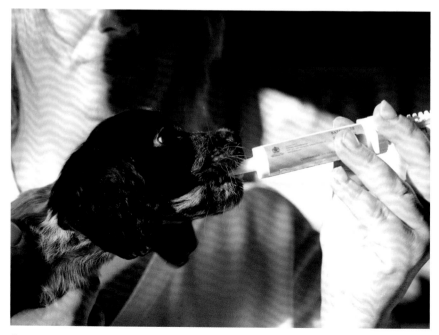

Paste wormers are easy to use.

transmitted via slugs and snails, which puppies may eat deliberately or by accident when licking bowls and toys left outdoors overnight. Your vet will be able to advise you on protecting your dog from this potentially very serious problem.

You may occasionally hear a dog owner stating that there is no need to worm your puppy. They may tell you that they have never wormed their dog and that he has never caught worms. Unfortunately, this is unlikely to be true, and it is impossible to tell whether or not a dog has a mild case of worms without testing his faeces in a laboratory.

Fleas, ticks and mites

External parasites can be troublesome, especially in the summer. It is important to keep your puppy free from fleas, not only because they make him uncomfortable, but because they can also infect him with tapeworms. A puppy that is being bitten by fleas will often scratch a lot and nibble the fur around the base of his tail. You may not see any fleas on him until the infestation is very bad, because fleas tend to bite the dog, then hide in his bedding or in your carpets.

Be very careful if you have a cat and decide to treat your puppy for fleas at home. Certain dog-flea treatments can make a cat very ill indeed. Just sharing a basket with a flea-treated dog can make a cat sick. Talk to your vet before treating your puppy.

Once your puppy is out and about in the countryside, ticks can be a nuisance and in some areas there is a risk of Lyme disease transmission. A swollen tick looks like a large grey pea in your dog's fur and feels quite firm. Check your puppy for ticks when you get home and use a tick remover to dislodge them. Don't apply chemicals or heat to the tick to make it let go because this may induce the animal to discharge its stomach contents into your dog, increasing the risk of infection. The sooner you get the tick off, the less likely it is to cause a problem.

Another unpleasant parasite problem is ear mites. These cause the puppy to shake his head repeatedly and his ears will look grubby inside. Aside from the horrible irritation that mites cause, the persistent ear flapping in longer-eared dogs can cause a blood-filled swelling in the ear flap itself. This may require a minor operation to fix and so it is well worth treating as soon as you notice a problem.

There are 'spot-on' chemicals that you put on your puppy to kill ticks and fleas, which carry on working for several weeks after application, although reports of resistance to some popular brands are growing. There are also 'spot-on' treatments that kill some worm infestations. Your vet will be able to recommend products and you can also find most good brands online.

Finding a vet

Recommendation from a friend or neighbour is a good starting place in your search for a vet. Failing that you will have to pick a local vet and see how you get on. Most veterinary surgeons are dedicated professionals who adore animals and are committed to your puppy's best interests. But you can always change to a different vet later on if you are not happy with your first choice.

When you take your puppy along for his first check-up, which should ideally be within a day or two of collecting him, you may be surprised to find that your vet suggests a date for neutering your new friend. Some veterinary surgeons, it must be said, have considerable enthusiasm for separating dogs from their reproductive equipment. This is for several reasons, including health advantages for the dog as well as for the more obvious birth-control purposes. Some of the health benefits to neutering are fairly significant, especially where bitches are concerned, but there are also some health disadvantages. We'll look at the question of neutering more closely in Part Three.

Your vet will be able to advise you on keeping your puppy free from fleas.

The cost of veterinary care

Veterinary science has kept pace with human medical science. Extraordinary advances have been made that were unthinkable when I was a child. But these advances have come at a price. Bills for veterinary treatment can run into many thousands of pounds. People without insurance may be in the desperate situation of having to choose between their dog's life and their daughter's college fund. One way to avoid this unhappy state of affairs is to take out veterinary insurance.

All insurance policies are not equal, and it is very important to read the small print. Some policies won't cover a working dog for example. Others will not automatically renew your insurance at the end of the year if your dog has developed a serious illness. This can be devastating if a dog needs expensive treatment, such as chemotherapy or major surgery, which falls outside the policy renewal date. A good policy, with adequate cover for expensive treatment and unconditional annual renewal, can save you a great deal of heartache in the future.

Together with the support of your vet, you should be able to keep your puppy in good physical health. You can also call upon your vet for advice should you have behavioural problems with your dog in the future. However, your best safeguard against problems with temperament and behaviour is to raise a confident and happy puppy.

The next step on this journey is to create a place in your home where your new puppy can feel safe. In the following chapter, we look at how you can create a comforting den that will help your puppy settle in without too much fuss and bother, and set him on the road to becoming a happy and well-adjusted companion.

SUMMARY

- Vaccination will protect your puppy against fatal diseases.
- Carry your puppy when out and about on socialisation trips until his vaccinations are complete.
- Regularly treat your puppy for parasites, internal and external.
- Consider taking out veterinary insurance.

7

A place of safety

We can only guess at how a new puppy feels when he leaves behind everything he has ever known and arrives in a brand new world. Although most new puppies are about eight weeks old when they leave home and still quite trusting of strangers, it is reasonable to assume that your puppy will miss his mother and his brothers and sisters for a while. Everything in your home must seem strange. All around him are new sights, new smells and new sounds. Without doubt, there is great potential for this little dog to feel very lost and lonely. The aim of this chapter is to help you settle your puppy in, and make him feel at home as quickly as possible.

There are two ways to make any tiny puppy feel safe and secure. One is to keep him very close to you; the other is to place him in his home den. Your problem, for the first few days, is that your puppy's home den is far away.

What is a home den?

The home den is not just a bed or basket where the puppy sleeps. It is much more than that. Your puppy's first den was the place where he first opened his eyes, where he was suckled by his mother, and where he slept with his siblings. As far as your puppy is concerned, this den is a place of absolute safety, even when his mother is not there. It is important to acknowledge that when you bring your puppy home, he will be leaving his home den behind.

One of your first priorities will be to recreate a den in your home as quickly as you can – a place where your puppy feels safe. This is easier said than done, because many of the attributes of a home den, familiarity, scent and sounds, cannot be manufactured. There are, however, some features of a home den that all puppies have a preference for, and you can help your puppy settle in by making sure these are available for him.

He may feel rather lost to begin with.

What does a home den look like?

Your idea of a great place to sleep and relax may be very different from your puppy's. A puppy likes small, dark, enclosed spaces. He is not bothered about the structure or the contents of the den, he is not overly impressed with fluffy blankets and designer duvets, and he has no natural fear of being confined; nor does he share our aversion to the gaol-like presence of bars.

Puppies chew anything and everything. So for his own safety, a den needs to be free from hazardous material that could be torn up and swallowed. Most breeds of dog are physically quite hardy and by eight weeks old, a healthy puppy can regulate his own temperature indoors without the need for extra heat, so you don't need to place his den against a radiator or provide a heat lamp. However, his den does need to be sufficiently airy, and free from draughts and damp. And in the summer it needs to be out of direct sunlight and in a room that stays reasonably cool.

Should you use a dog crate?

Although the use of dog crates is now widespread in the UK and beyond, you do still occasionally hear people say that they think it is cruel to put a dog in a crate.

Indeed, when dog crates were invented, I thought them an appalling idea. How could we put our friends in a cage!

Our own feelings about bars and cages are very much bound up in the value we place on liberty. A new puppy may cry and try to get out of a crate if you place him inside one and walk away. This is because puppies have a strong need

Providing him with a cosy den will help this puppy feel safe and happy.

to be near their grown-ups, not because they have any objections to having their liberty removed. It is likely that dogs do not have any understanding of an abstract concept such as freedom, and all the evidence points to dogs being perfectly happy in a crate that is used appropriately.

The advantages of crating

A puppy that has a crate to sleep in may feel at home sooner than a puppy that simply has a bed or basket placed out in the open space of a room in your house. You can make the crate cosier and more den-like for a small puppy by placing a blanket or old towel over one end. An appropriately sized crate represents that small confined space that puppies find so attractive and helps the puppy to accept this as his new home den.

Puppies have a strong instinct to keep their den clean. This means that within the limited capacity of their immature bladder and bowels, a puppy will not attempt to relieve himself in a small crate. He will wait until you take him outside. This is a massive help in establishing good house-training habits.

A crate will also help to keep your puppy safe when you cannot supervise him. A family home is full of hazards for a small puppy, from small items that might choke him or substances that might poison him, to being trodden on by clumsy humans or electrocuted when he chews through the refrigerator cable. It will also protect him from the wrath of family members as he will have less opportunity to destroy their prized possessions. In busy households, at busy times of the day, the crate is a place of safety and gives the puppy a safe space where he can relax when all around him is chaotic.

The disadvantages of crating

There is no doubt that crates have the potential to be abused. Dogs can be neglected and shut in them for far too long. It is probably true to say that this also applies to the alternatives to crates, although the small size of the crate amplifies this problem. Apart from at night, a puppy should never be left in a crate for long periods of time. The risk that he will become isolated and neglected, and fail to bond properly with his family, is too great.

If you decide to use a puppy crate, you will need to be disciplined about letting the puppy out frequently and not relying on it too much. Another downside with a crated puppy is that you will have to get up in the night to take the puppy out, until his bladder can hold a full night's urine. This may take from a few nights to a couple of weeks.

Now let's look at other ways of managing your small puppy in the absence of a crate.

Alternatives to crating

A puppy pen consists of a number of interlinking wire panels, usually five or six panels in all. It does not have a base and so should be placed on a washable floor. You put the puppy's bed in the pen, and cover the remaining floor area with newspaper or puppy pads. Most puppies will wee on the paper and not in the bed. There can be problems with puppy pens. Some puppies will rip up and play with the newspaper you have so carefully arranged, and wee or poo on the exposed floor beneath – a habit that you will need to break him of later. Your puppy might pull his bedding out of his basket onto the newspaper to play with, and it may then be dragged through anything that he has deposited there. Your puppy may also step in, play with, and possibly eat, his own faeces, which will not endear him to you, and which can also become a habit.

A two-door crate gives you a choice of positions.

House-training a pen-raised puppy can take longer than crate training, and you will need to be vigilant about keeping the floor of the pen clean. Of course, some puppies don't attempt to rearrange their pen and it is a system that works well for some families. One advantage *to you* of a puppy pen is that, because you can leave water down and he has somewhere to relieve himself, you can leave him for longer than you could if he were crated. This aspect of puppy pens is not necessarily an advantage for *puppies* because it can encourage owners to leave them alone for too long. For some reason, we seem to feel better about leaving a dog alone for a long time if we give him more space to be lonely in. It is important to remember that the dog doesn't care about space. He only cares about being with you.

Remember, to make the small puppy feel safe, it is best if his bed has some kind of roof. A small plastic carry crate with the door open placed inside the pen will suffice. A cardboard box on its side can work, although some puppies will destroy this within minutes.

A dedicated room for the puppy is another alternative, and this can work if you have a suitable utility room opening onto your kitchen. But again, you may have house-training problems, because the puppy will learn to empty himself indoors and you will then have to teach him not to. As you can see, this is not a straightforward decision. Overall, I feel that the advantages to the puppy of using a crate greatly outweigh the possible disadvantages, which can be avoided by thoughtful use.

Soft bedding is cosy, but watch out for chewing.

Choosing a crate

Most of the benefits of the crate are dependent on it being small enough, so that the puppy will quickly accept it as a den, and most importantly, will keep it clean. If you buy a crate that is too big, your puppy *will* wee at one end and sleep at the other, just as he would in a puppy pen.

Your puppy needs to be able to stand up in his crate without banging his head on the roof, and to turn around easily, or lie down on his side. A crate should have this much space and *not much more*. This means that you will need two crates. One for the first four months or so of your puppy's life, and another to last him until he is adult. Many dogs will need to be crated at night for up to a year to ensure they remain clean and dry in the house, and until they have outgrown any enthusiasm for chewing through your chair legs. So the second crate must be purchased with your puppy's adult size in mind. Some larger crates can be fitted with a divider that you can take out as the puppy grows; or it may be possible for you to borrow a small crate to last him for the first few months.

Accepting the crate

For the first few days, your puppy may well cry whenever you leave him alone. Initially, this crying will simply be because he feels unsafe. But if you inadvertently reward him for crying, he will rapidly learn to cry deliberately in order to get your attention. You can avoid this situation arising by making sure that you let the puppy out of the crate only when he is being quiet. You can find out more about how to achieve this in Chapter 21, 'The noisy puppy'.

The more times the puppy enters his den and nothing upsetting happens to him, the better. We can achieve this through frequently feeding the puppy inside the crate, and leaving little surprises in there for him – a cube of cheese or a chunk of roast chicken will go down well. An additional important factor in helping your new puppy to feel safe is making sure that he knows where his den is and that he can get at it easily and quickly whenever he wants to. This means initially restricting the puppy to a small part of your house, close to his den. There are other advantages in this strategy, too, and we will look at these in the chapter on house-training, Chapter 13, 'Clean and dry'.

It will take up to a week for your puppy to feel safe in the den you have provided for him. The more frequently he experiences being in the crate under pleasurable circumstances, the sooner he will accept it as his new home. Make his den a happy place, feed him often there, leave tasty Kongs in there for him to chew, and don't be tempted to shut him in for long periods of time. The crate should be his place of safety and not his prison. Little and often is the key to success.

As your puppy grows and matures, his need for a small den will diminish. Over the next few months he will grow to regard your entire house as his den. And when this process is complete, you will have a fully house-trained dog that is in every sense a part of your family.

SUMMARY

- Make a safe home den for your puppy.
- Choosing a crate has house-training advantages, but don't keep him in it for too long.
- Feeding him in his den will encourage him to accept it readily.
- Make sure the crate is the right size.
- Expect to get up in the night to begin with.

8

Puppy paperwork

Bringing a puppy into your life is not only an emotional and practical experience; it is a legal transaction and usually a significant financial one, too. There are rights and responsibilities on both sides, and some of these involve documentation. So before we move on to our next chapter and talk about making those final preparations for the arrival of your new puppy, let's take a look at the ins and outs of puppy paperwork. Some of this information may not apply to you if you are not buying a pedigree puppy, and which documents you need will depend on individual circumstances. There are four types of paperwork that you may need to understand and in some cases check *before* you collect your puppy.

- **Health certificates**
- **Registration documents**
- **Contract of sale**
- **Insurance and vaccination certificates**

Health certificates

It is crucial to check any relevant health clearances in advance of collecting your puppy. As soon as the puppy is in your arms, you will be emotionally committed to him. Many pedigree dog breeds have a range of known potential health issues for which responsible breeders test their breeding stock. Some breeders of cross-bred dogs (e.g. Labradoodles) also carry out these tests. The health checks for many breeds will include tests for hip dysplasia and various eye diseases. Some dog breeds are prone to metabolic problems, heart disease and so on. I cannot tell you which tests your dog should have as they vary widely from breed to breed, and also because the recommended tests may be added to or amended over time. It is really important that you find out which tests apply to your breed before

Pedigree puppies like these Italian Spinones come with paperwork.

purchasing your puppy. You can visit the Kennel Club website where you will find the relevant health issues for your particular breed. Bear in mind that it is usually the parents of your puppy that will have been tested, not the puppy itself. So you will need to see certificates for both his father and his mother. If you are buying a first cross, such as a Labradoodle, you should still make sure that each parent has the health clearances relevant to their breed, *especially* when the health issue in question is a known problem in *both* breeds.

Make sure that you know what a good result is. In many cases, the certificate will simply declare the parent dog is clear of a particular condition. In others, hip dysplasia for example, the certificate will give the dog a score and you need to know what is a good score for your breed. Again, this information is available on the Kennel Club website.

Let the buyer beware

Registration with the UK Kennel Club does *not*, at the time of writing, offer you a complete guarantee that puppies have been bred from parents that have no health problems. It is currently still possible for a breeder to register puppies that have been bred from parents that have health issues.

It really is a case of buyer beware. It is up to you to make sure that your puppy has been bred from healthy stock. Once you know which health clearances your puppy's parents should have passed, you need to ask the breeder to show you the certificates when you visit the puppies, or to send you some copies. These can be scanned or photographed and emailed to you. Whatever you do, don't skip this step. Some of the health conditions affecting domestic dogs are surprisingly common. They can empty your wallet in a heartbeat, and even if you are fully insured, they can blight your life for the next ten years or more. A sick or disabled dog can be a huge burden and a strain on family ties and relationships.

Registration documents

There is only one official body responsible for registering pedigree dogs in the UK and that is the Kennel Club. Many other countries have an official Kennel Club of their own, which similarly is the only official body for registering pedigree dogs in that country. The Kennel Club is a non-profit organisation and while it often comes in for some criticism, it does a huge amount of good for dogs. If you are buying a pedigree puppy, it must be registered with the Kennel Club. Do not be misled by pedigrees or registration documents from alternative registries. There are currently a number of websites running registration systems that look quite official. They charge a fee and post their 'pedigree' documents to breeders who, for some reason or another, have elected not to register with the Kennel Club. These are not genuine KC registrations and so have no value in the eyes of most breeders and puppy buyers, and may cause you great disappointment in the future.

If at any time in your puppy's life you wish to breed from him, or decide to participate in some of the activities organised by the KC, you will need genuine KC registration papers. At the time of writing, any breeder of *pedigree* dogs who is registering with one of these alternative bodies probably has something to hide.

Kennel Club registration is subject to some restrictions that protect our dogs. Breeders may not register puppies from bitches over a certain age with the Kennel Club, or if the bitch has had more than the maximum number of allowed litters. These regulations are aimed at protecting dogs from over-breeding. You can see why breeders who break these regulations might be tempted to register their puppies elsewhere.

When your puppy was born, he will have been registered in his breeder's name. It is then up to you to inform the Kennel Club that ownership has been transferred. You can do this using the registration document, which your breeder must give you when you collect your puppy. Many breeders will also have purchased, and will give you, a five-generation pedigree certificate, which will show you your puppy's family tree. If not, you can purchase one of these from the Kennel Club when you transfer ownership of the puppy.

Some breeders are quite slow about registering their puppies and may not have the registration certificate ready for you when you collect your pup. This is not ideal and you will need to decide whether you are prepared to take the puppy on trust. Breeders may also choose to include endorsements on the registration of your puppy. But what does this mean to you?

He may look like a picture of health but be sure to check his certificates.

Endorsements

Endorsements are stipulations that the breeder has made regarding any attempts that you may make to breed from your puppy in the future. These stipulations cannot prevent you breeding from your dog, but they can prevent you registering any litters you produce with the Kennel Club, so they must be taken seriously.

The purpose of these endorsements is to give the breeder some control over what happens to the puppies she has bred, and to ensure that their descendants will be healthy.

In order to register any puppies you breed from your dog, you will need to get the endorsement lifted. This can happen only with the agreement of the person who placed the endorsement in the first place. Such agreement may not be unreasonably withheld, and provided that you carry out the relevant health checks, the endorsement will be removed.

Contract of sale

When you hand over a puppy in exchange for money, a contract of sale exists between you and the breeder. Many breeders will also supply you with a paper contract of sale. This does not normally detract from your legal rights and may add to them.

A contract of sale is usually fairly brief and may include an undertaking by your breeder to take your puppy back if at any time you are unable to look after it. Some contracts may even insist that you return the puppy in these circumstances, although this may not be enforceable. Once you have paid for the puppy, in the eyes of the law, he is now your property. A contract must also include information about any endorsements that the breeder has added when registering the puppy. Without this information the endorsements are likely to be invalid.

There is no harm in asking to see a copy of your breeder's standard contract in advance of collecting your puppy. That way, you can check out or clarify any item that you are not comfortable with before the big day.

Insurance and vaccination certificates

You don't need to view vaccination and insurance documents in advance of collecting your puppy – indeed, there may not be any. Many puppies are not vaccinated at the time of purchase, and this is perfectly acceptable.

Kennel Club registered puppies normally come with a few weeks' free insurance. The insurance company will normally remind you when this is about to expire, but it is probably a good idea to make a note in your diary. You may, of course, wish to use a different insurance company, but do check the small print of any insurance policy thoroughly.

Final preparations

I have given you quite a lot to think about over the last few chapters. Much of what we have talked about has been focused on health. The fact is, there are no guarantees of a healthy puppy, but the steps you take in arming yourself with information, and double checking the credentials of your dog's parents, are all in order to shorten the odds against you.

Once you have done all you can do, it is time to stop worrying and get ready to enjoy your dog. Our next, and final, chapter in Part One will help you make sure that your home and garden is prepared for your new arrival, and that you have purchased all the equipment you need to get you through the next few weeks without stress or strain.

SUMMARY

- Check that your puppy's parents have clean bills of health.
- Check a pedigree puppy is registered on the Kennel Club's breed register.
- Endorsements are a way of safeguarding the puppy.
- Look at your breeder's standard contract of sale before collecting your puppy.

9

Final preparations

The moment you have been waiting for is drawing near. You have almost completed your preparations for the arrival of your puppy. In Part Two of this book we will be looking at the practicalities of living with your puppy and keeping him happy, healthy and safe on a daily basis. In the meantime, as the big day approaches, it's time to check that you have everything you need, and to make sure everything is in place to ensure that the arrival of your puppy goes smoothly.

Let's look first at some of the purchases you will need to make.

In the home

Until house-training is well under way, you will need to restrict your puppy from unsupervised access to parts of the house that are carpeted. You will probably want to prevent him from going upstairs, too, as climbing steps at a very young age has been associated with joint problems.

You can now purchase baby gates online fairly inexpensively and you may be able to find second-hand ones at car-boot sales or online. If you buy second-hand, make sure the gates have all four large screws that attach to each corner. These are needed to brace the gate against the walls, and are easily lost when old gates are packed away. For a very small puppy, you may want to attach a fine mesh wire to the gate itself to prevent him from squeezing between the bars, or put a board across the bottom.

Most cats can walk between the bars of a baby gate or jump easily over the top, so this also makes a nice barrier through which the cat can escape when he has had enough of being bounced on and licked.

You will also need to purchase or borrow a puppy crate to fit your puppy for the first four months. If in doubt, the crate supplier will be able to advise you on size.

Crate supply is a very competitive business and crates have come down in price significantly over the years, so you shouldn't need to spend a fortune. If you decide against a crate, or are intending to allow the puppy access to any of your rooms unsupervised, you need to barricade off any electric cables securely. It takes a puppy just seconds to bite through one.

Purchasing a bed

Many puppies chew everything and have *no* respect for soft furnishings. *Any* bedding, toys or cushions that you put into your puppy's crate will probably be damaged. Don't be tempted to spend a small mortgage on a designer dog duvet. It is unlikely to survive the first night. The contents or stuffing will drift around your home for days and may cause problems if your puppy swallows some. Most puppies normally do well on vetbed. This is a kind of fleece on a roll that you can buy by the metre. Puppies are less likely to chew it than many other fabrics. It allows moisture to pass through in the event of an accident and stays dry and cosy. It is also machine washable and tumble dryable.

Car crates come in a range of styles.

Death-wish puppies!

If you are very unlucky, your puppy may rip up vetbed, too, and even swallow chunks of it. There are some puppies that just seem to be intent on swallowing everything in sight, a habit that can easily result in a trip to the local animal hospital for some major abdominal surgery. If your puppy turns out to be this way inclined, then you are going to have to find an alternative to bedding in his sleeping area.

You can line the tray of your crate with a tightly fitting piece of hard cow matting (available from agricultural suppliers), or even wooden board, such as plywood. This seems harsh, but both these are quite warm surfaces to sleep on. If it upsets you to see your puppy sleeping on a hard surface, bear in mind that your puppy will survive without a cosy bed, whereas some puppies will not survive an operation to remove a stomach blockage. Happily, this phase will pass. But until it does, you need to keep an eye on your pup and take whatever precautions are necessary to make sure he doesn't eat his way through your insurance premiums.

In the car

A boisterous puppy rampaging around your car while you are driving is extremely distracting. Small dogs can also get under the pedals and prevent you braking or operating your clutch. And in an accident, an unrestrained dog can become a missile. So for safety's sake, your puppy will need a secure place to travel in your vehicle. You can buy dog guards, which fit behind the rear seats and prevent the dog leaving the luggage area of your estate car or hatchback. However, these do not protect the *interior* of the luggage area from your puppy's sharp teeth and from his urgent need to chew. Car crates are a better option.

Travel crates can be purchased in a huge range of styles, and you will almost certainly be able to get one that fits neatly in the rear of an estate car. Saloon cars can be more problematic, and you may end up using a smaller carry crate initially, then transitioning to a dog harness on the back seat later. This isn't ideal, because some dogs will chew everything in sight, including the harness, your upholstery and anything else within reach, until well past their first birthday. You might want to give this some thought because a harness will not protect your car from damage. Many new dog owners end up trading in their saloon for an estate or hatchback.

While we are on the topic of cars, I must add a note of caution. Each summer in the UK and abroad, a number of dogs die horrific deaths inside cars, which have reached high temperatures when exposed to the sun. In most cases, the owners of the dog thought it couldn't happen to them. They had left the car for just a few minutes, or the weather was overcast, or they had parked in the shade. Be aware that leaving your puppy in a car once you have parked up, even in the safety of his crate, is potentially very dangerous. You could be waylaid or have an accident. While you are away the sun might come out, or the shade be lost. Don't let this happen to you. You would never forgive yourself. Be aware, too, that at any time of year, dog thieves may decide to help themselves to your beautiful puppy.

In the garden

Before your puppy arrives, you need to decide where he is going to go to the toilet. This outdoor space needs to be puppy-proof. You do not want to be chasing your puppy around your neighbour's garden with a torch at 3 a.m. because you didn't fix the hole in the fence.

Puppies can squeeze through smaller spaces than you might imagine. Some puppies are pretty good climbers, too. So make sure there is nothing against the fence that your puppy can use as a climbing aid to assist him in clambering

Puppies love gardening.

Move your tubs, or he will likely re-design the contents.

over the top. Some puppies have the excavating capabilities of a mechanical digger, so don't be tempted to leave your puppy outside unsupervised if there is no hard surface to prevent him tunnelling under the fence. And hedges, even thick ones, are not an obstacle to a puppy left to his own devices for very long.

If you intend to allow your puppy the freedom of your garden, the entire perimeter needs to be secure, and you need to think about puppy-proofing what is inside it. Check that the puppy will not be able to get into the garden shed and pull a spade on top of himself, or help himself to your slug bait.

Puppies love 'gardening' – especially digging and pruning. Unfortunately, their enthusiasm for the job is not matched by any kind of natural ability in the landscaping and plant-care department. Think about what you are going to do with any planters or tubs, and do consider how the puppy might affect any flowerbeds or vegetable plots that you are fond of. Anything you leave in the puppy's outdoor area will be treated as fair game. As well as flowerbeds, tubs and planters, this includes garden furniture, watering cans and hosepipes. Don't be tempted to set yourself up for weeks of conflict where the puppy repeatedly tries to wreck your stuff and dig up your petunias while you repeatedly try to stop him. That way madness lies.

With a very large garden, it may be impractical to attempt to puppy-proof the entire area. In this case, you may find it helpful to buy or build a temporary enclosure or puppy playpen. This means you can put your puppy down in the pen while you hang up the washing or do some gardening, without having to watch him like a hawk. If you are undecided where to place your playpen, bear in mind that puppies often prefer to wee on grass. You may get off to a quicker start with house-training if you allow your puppy access to an area of grass when you take him outside.

I don't want this to be a chapter of doom, but sadly there is another warning I should make at this point. Dog theft is not uncommon in the UK, and not just from vehicles. Puppies are a great target for dog thieves because they are so saleable. So don't be tempted to leave a puppy in a playpen in your garden while you pop out to the shops, even if he cannot be seen from the road. He just might not be there when you return.

You are going to be spending time outside with your puppy, day and night, so some light, and a chair, can be useful. Solar-powered garden lights on a spike that you push into the grass can provide just enough light for you to keep an eye on your puppy when he needs a wee in the night, without disturbing your neighbours' beauty sleep. A reliable torch may also come in handy for your night-time manoeuvres.

Toys and training aids

The most important toys you can buy for your puppy are Kongs. A Kong is a hollow and heavy rubber toy, which is extremely resistant to damage from chewing. Kongs come in a range of sizes, so you can start out with a puppy Kong and work your way up as he grows. You will need three puppy Kongs to begin with. One for him to chew, one for you to wash, and a third to be filled with food and frozen.

Toys need to be tough.

You give the puppy the frozen Kong when you have to leave him alone for a while. This fulfils his need to chew and keeps him from getting bored and miserable. You then pack the centre of one of your spares with soft food and freeze it.

Rawhide chews are another chewing toy and, in theory, are edible. However, they make many dogs sick when the bits are swallowed, and a puppy must never be left alone with one as he could choke on the pieces that he pulls off. Rawhide chews and rawhide bones are ideal for keeping a puppy occupied while he is cuddled on your lap, and a diversion from biting your fingers. You hang on to one end of the chew while he gnaws at the other.

You can buy all manner of soft squashy toys for puppies and *some* puppies love them and treat them gently. Those puppies usually belong to someone else, and most of the puppies I have raised have made short work of destroying anything remotely cuddly with deadly efficiency. Death-wish puppies will add a nice fat vet bill to the cost of the toy. Be wary of softer rubber toys and inspect them frequently for damage and loose bits. Big sturdy knotted ropes are usually quite hard-wearing and most puppies like carrying them around and gnawing at them.

Like children, puppies soon lose interest in familiar toys, so keep some by, out of sight, to amuse him when he is bored with his current favourites.

All puppies should learn to retrieve and for this you will need a ball or retrieving dummy. Kept out of the puppy's reach and used only when you are interacting with him, these special toys will retain their novelty value and hold your puppy's interest. Balls need to be small enough to fit in the puppy's mouth but far too big to swallow. So you may need to discard old balls as he outgrows them and they become a choking hazard. Most puppies can pick up larger balls than you might expect.

Slippers!

Puppies like to chase, grab and bite anything that is moving around at floor level. This includes your feet. In the next section of this book I will explain how to resolve the biting problem, but this takes a little time. In the meantime, if you don't have any slippers, I strongly recommend you buy some now. This is especially important for young children, who will quickly be reduced to tears as your tiny furry bundle transforms himself into a crocodile and pursues them around the kitchen. Try not to be tempted with anything very fluffy as any moving fluffy object will be incredibly attractive to a puppy. Rubber-soled slippers will also be handy when you have to take your puppy into the garden in the small hours.

A new game for your children

If you have children, this is a good time to stock up on some new and absorbing toys and books. Buy that latest game they have been longing for. Don't give it to them yet; put it away and save it for after the puppy arrives. Children can be very intense with new puppies and it is often helpful to have something to hand that deflects their attention away from the new arrival for a while.

Doggy day-care

If you intend to go back to work full time during your dog's lifetime, you will need to consider in advance how you will make arrangements for his comfort and welfare.

It is beyond the scope of this book to advise you on whether you should or should not own a dog. But remember that a crate is not a suitable long-term solution for a dog left alone during the day on a regular basis. Other than at night, you cannot crate a small puppy for hours at a time. He will simply become miserable and/or learn to mess in his crate. If you have to leave your puppy on a regular basis, you have two alternatives. You can arrange for someone else to attend to his needs while you are away, or you can provide him with a proper outdoor kennel with a run.

A properly constructed kennel has a place where a dog can stretch his legs, a place where he can relieve himself, and a sleeping area where he has shelter from the wind, sun and rain. There are, however, major drawbacks to kennelling a puppy on his own. Dogs are social animals and may become miserable if left alone for long periods of time. Many dogs take to barking repeatedly in order to keep themselves company. If you want to stay on speaking terms with your neighbours, this needs to be considered. A kennel run also needs to be well screened from public view or you will find your dog developing a passion for barking furiously at everyone who passes by. Kennelling has so many disadvantages for a small puppy that the best option for most families is to find some form of day-care.

As more and more couples work full time, the number of people who look after other people's dogs during the day while the owners are at work has grown. You can find dog walkers in most areas. These are people whom you pay to come in during the day while you are at work to let your dog out or take him for a walk. You might want to think about booking one of these in advance if you plan to return to work while your puppy is small.

A place in a good crèche will give your puppy the opportunity to play with other dogs.

If you live in or near a city or large town, you may also have access to a dog crèche where you can drop your dog off on your way to work and collect him on your way home. Good crèches may get booked up, so it is well worth thinking about this in advance.

Another alternative is an arrangement with a friend, relative or neighbour, but just like childcare, this can work well in some situations and cause bad feeling in others.

Choosing a collection date

Routines play an important part in keeping puppies contented, and the establishment of a new home den for your puppy is the first key to his happiness. So it is a very bad idea to collect a puppy when there is a lot going on in your life. All good breeders will hold on to a puppy for a week or two rather than have it go to a new home at a difficult time.

Don't be tempted to collect your puppy on Christmas Eve, or the day before your daughter's wedding. And don't take a tiny puppy on holiday with you. You won't be able to settle him in properly and he is highly likely to become stressed and unwell.

Your puppy is going to need your undivided attention for some time. If you work full time, it is a good idea to book your annual leave in time to spend it with your new arrival.

Life is about to change

If you have never owned a dog before, and your puppy has not yet arrived, you will be aware that you are about to begin an exciting new chapter in your life. Nothing will ever be quite the same again.

Unless you have small children, life without a puppy tends to be relatively civilised. You can get up when you want to, go out for as long as you want to, take weekend breaks or book a last-minute bargain holiday. Within reason, you can do whatever you want, whenever you want to do it. You can leave cupcakes on your coffee table, and bacon on the kitchen unit, in the knowledge that it will still be there in ten minutes' time. No one will disassemble your shoes or chew a hole in your favourite sweater if you forget to put them away. And the chances are no one ever leaves suspicious puddles on your kitchen floor, or underneath your bed.

Your world is about to change. But don't panic. Many of the adjustments you will need to make in your life to accommodate this new family member are just temporary, and are easily dealt with by anyone who is well prepared. Puppies grow up very quickly. And the permanent changes that we make to accommodate them in our lives are, for most of us, a worthwhile trade-off for the many joys and benefits of owning a dog.

The next part of this book is intended to guide you through the first few weeks with your puppy. We begin by looking at your very first day together, and cover each of the major hurdles that you will need to overcome as you get to know your new friend. Let's move on now to the big day – collecting your puppy.

SUMMARY AND CHECKLIST

Have you:

- Bought a crate, car crate and baby gates?
- Bought vetbedding to fit the crates?
- Bought some Kongs, a rope toy and a ball or two?
- Puppy-proofed an outside area or bought a puppy pen for the garden?
- Set up some garden lights where necessary?
- Bought a torch and some slippers?
- Arranged a puppy-sitter for when you go back to work?
- Bought a game for your kids?
- Stocked up on familiar food (the same brand as used by your breeder)?
- Booked an appointment with your vet the day after your puppy arrives?

Part Two

Life with your puppy

10

Collecting your puppy

A t last the big day has arrived. The waiting is over and it is time to collect the new addition to your family. The day that you bring home your puppy is a fairly momentous occasion. You are about to begin a new chapter in your life and you are bound to feel excited, and perhaps just a little anxious.

We all have our own way of doing things. If you like to organise every outing like a military manoeuvre, as I do, you won't need me to remind you to make a list and plan the day carefully. If, on the other hand, you are a free spirit, who likes to take things as they come, I suggest you read through this chapter first. My objective is to help your day go smoothly. We'll look at the best way to travel with a small puppy, what you need to take with you, and what you will need to bring home with you in addition to your new friend.

Before you leave the house, you'll need to prepare your puppy's den and put up any baby gates that you are going to use. Have the puppy's crate ready in a family room with a washable floor. Put baby gates across any doorways into carpeted rooms. If you are intending to use a puppy playpen for your puppy's outdoor toilet area, put this up before you leave. You don't want to be juggling a puppy with one hand, and trying to put up a playpen with the other.

Make a checklist of everything you want to take with you, and pack the car. It is a good idea to set off in plenty of time. There may be other people arriving at the breeder's home that day to collect puppies from the same litter, and she will hopefully have staggered arrival times so that she can give each family her full attention. Try to arrive at the agreed time, even if it means stopping on the way for a coffee in order to avoid being early. As well as this helping the breeder, it means that you get a good share of her attention and it is less likely that something important will be forgotten. If you have another dog, it is a good idea to leave him at home or with a friend for this particular trip. Having him along may complicate things.

What to take with you

The journey home will be much simpler if you take a friend to help you. You will need a travel crate of some description in case you have to restrain the puppy in the vehicle (more details below). Line the crate with vetbedding or an old towel. Take a travel pack with a couple of bin bags (to put soiled waste in), spare newspaper, a spare towel and plenty of baby wipes. It is probably a good idea not to wear your best clothes! If this all sounds a bit ominous, don't panic – not all puppies are carsick but if you prepare yourself in this way, the worst that can happen is that you will need your kit. Hopefully, you will be lucky and have an uneventful journey home.

Take with you a list of notes/questions that you want to ask the breeder. If your visit overlaps with someone else's, or she is very busy, things can easily be forgotten. Note down any documents you need to see, and make a note to ask the breeder when the puppy was last fed, when he was last wormed and whether or not he has been vaccinated. Don't forget to take the breeder's phone number in case you get lost! You will also need to take payment for the puppy in the form agreed with the breeder. Many breeders will not take a cheque on the day of collection but will want it to have cleared through their bank first.

When you arrive at the breeder's home, you will usually be offered a cup of tea and an opportunity to go over the puppy's routine and your puppy paperwork. Check out Chapter 8, 'Puppy paperwork', in Part One so that you know in advance what documents you will be given and which documents you should ask to see.

What to collect from the breeder

If you are buying a pedigree puppy, make sure that the breeder gives you the registration certificate, and the pedigree certificate, and make sure that they are for the same puppy! Check that the KC registration numbers match. Your breeder has probably registered several puppies and it is an easy mistake to mix up documents. If the puppies have had their first vaccination, you will need your puppy's vaccination certificate, too. Many puppies will not have been vaccinated at all, and that is perfectly alright. You can read up on vaccinations in Part One if you haven't done so already. Don't forget to check the relevant health certificates if you haven't seen them already.

Some breeders will give you a little piece of blanket or vetbed to take with you so that the puppy has something with the smell of home on it. Don't forget

Leaving home is a big step for this little Springer Spaniel puppy.

to take some of the puppies familar food with you. Breeders normally give you enough for several days. Some breeders will give you a puppy pack with food samples, leaflets and lots of information and advice, all provided by the food manufacturer.

What to expect on the journey home

The chances are that your puppy has never been in a car before. He has also never been away from the home where he was born and where he feels safe. If you put your puppy in a crate in the back of your car and drive home with him shut in there, one or all of the following three things may happen.

- He will scream very loudly most of the way.
- He will be sick.
- He will empty his bowels.

This is simply because the puppy is stressed and feels abandoned. He may be perfectly safe in the crate in the event of an accident, but your driving is likely to be adversely affected by the noise and the smell. All in all, it is not a very good start to his new life.

For this reason, when I collect a puppy, I always take an adult passenger with me, or get someone else to drive. Then the puppy can sit in the footwell on the passenger side of the car. Pressed up against someone's legs, he will feel safe and won't scream with fear. It is the screaming and stress that tend to make the puppy move his bowels during the journey. Transported this way, most puppies sleep for at least part of the journey and don't get too upset. He may still be sick, though, from the motion of the vehicle.

Line the footwell of your car with newspaper and cover with an old towel. If you have a long journey home, the puppy may wet himself. Don't be tempted to put the puppy down *outside* the car because he is being sick. You just have to deal with any mess inside the car, if and when it happens – another reason why you need a helping hand.

You should also have a crate in the car ready and prepared for the puppy, in case you need it. Occasionally, a puppy will not settle in the footwell of the car, cries constantly and does his best to leap all over the front seats. This is unusual, but it can happen and it is very distracting for the driver. This is why you must have a crate ready in the car. Pull over in a safe place, transfer the puppy to the crate and complete the journey with him in there.

Arriving home

At last. You have made it home with your precious new bundle. You pull into the drive and switch off the engine. What now?

The very first thing you need to do is take the puppy straight to his outdoor toilet area so that he can have a wee. Offer him a drink of water and make yourself comfortable. It may take him a while to decide that it's okay to wee in this new place.

Puppies vary in how they react to being placed on the ground in a strange place. Some are like little clockwork toys – you put them on the ground and off they go. Others will be more hesitant, and a few will freeze with fear. If your puppy seems worried, get right down on the ground with him, let him know that you are there for him and let him climb on your lap if he wants to, while he

Your puppy may want to stay very close at first.

surveys this new world. He will want to stay near you but he will soon begin to sniff about and hopefully will decide to do a wee. Once he has emptied his bladder, you can take him indoors, but it is a good idea to set an alarm to remind you to take him back to his toilet area in half an hour's time. With all the excitement of his arrival and getting to know your new friend, the time will fly past.

So much fun ahead!

One step at a time

Stepping inside the door with a new puppy is a little bit like coming home with a new baby. For weeks or months you have thought about and prepared for this wonderful occasion. Now the moment is here, you may realise that you have invested so much in this one day that you have not really thought much about the days to come. You may feel a bit overwhelmed, or even a sense of anticlimax. But that's okay. We'll take it one step at a time. For now, you have a little while in which your puppy is unlikely to need another wee. It's time for some introductions.

SUMMARY
- Prepare your puppy's den, and put up baby gates and a playpen in the garden.
- Take someone with you to collect your puppy.
- Take a travel kit in case of carsickness.
- Check numbers match on registration and pedigree certificates.
- Take your puppy home travelling in the footwell of the car, pressed up against your passenger's legs.
- Put him in his toilet area as soon as you arrive home and every half-hour afterwards.

11

Making introductions

Over the next day or two, your puppy will be meeting, and getting to know, the members of his new family, and familiarising himself with his new home. It may be tempting to take your puppy on a grand tour of the neighbourhood, or to allow him to explore the entire house. But right now, he is probably feeling overwhelmed by just how very new everything is. For the time being, it is a good idea just to introduce him to his crate, and the room where you have placed it. Together with exploring his outdoor toilet area, this is probably enough for your little pup to take in during the first few days. Let him trot about, explore your kitchen and find his crate – leave the door open so he can go in and out. Ask your children and other family members to come into this room if they want to spend time with the puppy, rather than carting him off to their bedrooms where he will get up to all kinds of mischief!

Smaller children need to hold the puppy sitting down.

Meeting the family is what this chapter is about, and if you have children, they will definitely be at the front of the queue.

Meeting the children

Small children will be desperate to cuddle the puppy, but may need a little help. Show them how to hold the puppy gently on their laps while sitting down.

This Labrador puppy is being held safely with her weight supported in both arms.

Explain that the puppy may be feeling a bit lost and that they need to speak quietly and handle him calmly with very gentle stroking. Teaching children to handle puppies calmly and quietly is important. Small puppies can easily get very over-excited, and in this state they are likely to start nipping and being generally rather manic. We will talk about helping children to play safely with puppies later on, but for now he is a huge novelty and they will naturally want to hold him and get to know him.

Older children who are permitted to carry the puppy must be shown how to do this correctly, with his weight supported on one arm and the other arm wrapped protectively around him.

Once they have said hello and had a cuddle, now may be a good time to give smaller children a present that will engross them. A new DVD or video game will help take attention away from the puppy without you having to nag at the children to leave him in peace.

Meeting the cat

If you have a cat, he will probably think you have taken leave of your senses bringing a puppy into the house, and may well make himself scarce for a few days while he assesses the situation. Move his food and water into another room so that the puppy doesn't devour it, and so that the cat is not forced to run the puppy gauntlet in order to get a drink. Provided your cat is not trapped in the room with the puppy, he will probably start to observe and interact with the puppy in a day or two. You can help by giving the cat plenty of opportunity to leave the room whenever he chooses. Don't try to force the friendship, or the cat may choose to leave home for good!

Sometimes a different problem arises. Some cats are quite bold in the way that they approach puppies. In this case, the interaction between them must be carefully supervised. Cats can give a puppy a nasty facial scratch, and a scratched eye can be serious. Cats have also occasionally been known to kill very tiny puppies, so if you have a toy breed, be especially vigilant for the first few days.

The start of a new friendship.

It is important to remember that most cats and dogs end up getting along just fine, so give your cat plenty of space and let the friendship form naturally over time.

Your older dog

Older dogs vary widely in their initial reactions to puppies, and just like your cat, the older dog needs to be able to escape from your youngster when he wants to.

Although reactions vary, the majority of adult dogs have an instinctive set of behaviours that they display towards puppies they consider to be part of the family. I can't promise your dog will fall into this majority, but it is likely that he will. There is a set of rules, which most older dogs apply to known puppies.

- Rule one: puppies under four months old can do *whatever they want* and the older dog will not retaliate.
- Rule two: if a puppy wants to play, the older dog will join in for short periods of time, even if he never normally plays with other dogs.
- Rule three: puppies over four months can be disciplined mildly.
- Rule four: puppies over six months lose their right to special treatment.

Eight-week-old puppies treat all older dogs as playmates. They are programmed this way. Older dogs, however, may vary in the way that they respond. Fortunately, in most cases, rule one will keep your puppy safe.

Rule one

Rule one is a universal law that is understood by most healthy adult dogs. It gives a puppy a huge amount of licence to bite, tug and generally harass an older dog without any retaliation whatsoever. Some adult dogs are so tolerant that they will apply rule one to all puppies, but in many cases, the rule applies only to puppies that are members of the older dog's own social group. This means that it may take a few days for rule one to kick in and protect your puppy. In the meantime, you may need to supervise very closely indeed.

A new puppy is not good at reading subtle signals from older dogs and may be unable to distinguish friendly older dogs from those that do not have good intentions towards him. You are going to have to do this on his behalf.

Let's play

In many cases, the very first thing a puppy will do when he meets an older dog is attempt to engage him in play. Older dogs vary in their reactions, but tend to fall into one of the following camps.

- The babysitter
- The big brother
- The distant uncle
- The grumpy grandpa

If your dog is socially competent (i.e. he knows the four puppy rules) and recognises the puppy as a member of your family, what you will see will gladden your heart. Your adult dog will perform some play bows where he goes down on his elbows with his bottom in the air. He will then probably lie down on the floor so that the puppy can reach his head, and he will mouth play with the puppy. This involves lots of fake growling and pretend grabbing, but the whole process takes place with the adult dog's mouth wide open. His demeanour will be happy, his tail gently wagging, and it will be clear that he knows what he is doing. Interaction between the two of them needs some supervision initially, but in time this dog may be your best babysitter. This may happen immediately, or after a space of two to three days once the puppy smells like the rest of you.

Your older dog may turn out to be your best babysitter.

Rough play!

The big brother is another common reaction to puppies and one that you tend to find in dogs that are themselves still quite immature. This dog thinks your puppy is absolutely *brilliant*. He just wants to play and play, but he is far too rough and keeps bowling the puppy over. He doesn't mean any harm and backs off, tail wagging, when the puppy squeals. But there is potential for damage here, at least until the puppy grows big enough to hold his own.

Once the puppy has grown a little, he will have great fun with his new big brother, but until then you are going to have to supervise quite closely and restrict interaction between them to a few minutes at a time.

This older dog is happy to play – her mouth is wide open and her front legs are bent.

This older dog is not comfortable with the puppy.

Go away

The distant uncle is not interested in other people's kids. He is quite clear in his own mind that this puppy is not a member of the family and should be regarded with suspicion. He will remain standing up in the proximity of the puppy, keeping still, and may stiffen his body and growl as the puppy approaches. This is a fairly common reaction and most dogs that behave in this way will warm to the puppy in time.

Grumpy grandpa

Old dogs have special dispensation. Some will play with puppies but many will not, even if they tolerate a certain amount of biting and pulling from the little one. The grumpy grandpa may be rather hard on a puppy when warning him off, or in some cases the puppy may bully the old dog until he cries pitifully. In either case, you will need to make sure your old friend has his own space.

Warning signs

Some dogs, for a range of reasons, are not socially competent. A socially incompetent dog does not know the puppy rules and will struggle to cope when the puppy tries to engage him in play. He may well be very afraid of the puppy and may overreact when the puppy hurts him. Like the distant uncle, he will remain standing up and may stiffen his body and growl as the puppy approaches, but in this case, his reaction to the puppy may be more aggressive and potentially dangerous. He may never actually want to play with the puppy. You will need to supervise this dog with special care until the puppy has learned to leave him in peace. As the puppy grows up, the friendship between them can then develop on an even footing.

Although some dogs may find puppies irritating, severe aggression towards puppies is not common. I think you can see that the key to success is supervision along with provision for the older dog to escape from the puppy when he has had enough. Even the best-natured dog may lose his temper with a puppy if he is constantly pestered and unable to escape, while the big brother may want to continue long after the puppy is completely exhausted. Your job is to be the referee, and this is easiest to achieve if each dog has his own space. At least to begin with.

Introducing mealtimes

Until the age of about three months, puppies need four meals a day. You should divide your puppy's daily rations between these meals, and time the meals so that the last one is well before your bedtime. This gives you the best chance of the puppy not needing to empty his bowels during the night.

Here's an example of a typical feeding routine.

- 7 a.m.   breakfast
- 11 a.m.   lunch
- 3 p.m.   tea
- 7 p.m.   supper

On your puppy's first day, he may well have missed one of these meals. This won't hurt him, and it is best not to try to top him up at the remaining mealtimes as that might upset his tummy. You don't need to starve your puppy, or give him extra, just because he has been carsick. He will recover from that very quickly.

It is important that you don't try, at any time, to cram extra meals into fewer, larger helpings, even though your puppy may seem quite capable of consuming the entire day's rations in one go. The impact of an overly large meal on his immature digestion is usually an unpleasant case of diarrhoea. However, it is fine to break his daily ration into even smaller portions.

In fact, you don't need to give the puppy all of his meal in a bowl at mealtimes. You can, and should, use part or even all of his meals as training aids. Food is a great comforter for puppies and is a useful training tool.

🐾 Introducing the crate

In Part One, we talked about creating a place of safety (Chapter 7) and setting up a cosy crate for your puppy to use as a den. One of our first priorities with a new puppy is to help him feel at home in his new den. The passage of time is a great settler and even if you take no steps to help him, he will get used to his crate over the next few days. However, there is much you can do to speed up this process.

Each time your puppy enters the crate it becomes more familiar to him. If each of these times is accompanied by a pleasant experience, the crate rapidly becomes associated with pleasure. Instead of feeding your puppy his first few meals from a bowl, put his allocated ration for each meal in a handy container and repeatedly take a few pieces from the container and place them in the crate. In this way, your puppy could have fifty or even a hundred, happy crate experiences before bedtime. This is particularly important if you are planning on leaving him alone in the crate on his first night.

Once the puppy is going in and out of his crate happily for food, you can begin to close the door from time to time. Do this very briefly to begin with. A few seconds is sufficient. Build a strong association between being crated, and food. Make sure the being *released* from the crate is associated with silence. Releasing a whimpering puppy from his crate will reinforce the whimpering. This is why it is so important to make being in the crate a happy experience from the very beginning.

Lots of snacks in the crate will help your puppy feel happy there.

The days ahead

The next few weeks are going to be pretty hectic. You have three major tasks to achieve all at the same time.

- Getting your puppy settled and sleeping at night
- House-training him
- Socialising him

It would be great if we could focus on just one of these things in the first week, another in the next week and another in the third, using a week-by-week guide. But unfortunately, we cannot. We have to tackle all these issues *at once*. If we don't settle the puppy in properly, we will have problems with crying or whining. If we don't start off on the right foot with house-training, we may have a puppy that messes in the house for many weeks. Likewise, if we don't get going with socialisation, we can end up with a nervous or even aggressive dog on our hands. So there is no way around it. We have to work on all three at the same time. But don't worry; you are going to manage just fine.

I suggest you read through the next few chapters in turn, and then come back to the relevant chapters as and when you need to.

Just like any new parents, getting your puppy to sleep happily through the night is an important milestone. For many new puppy owners it is a milestone that is achieved within the first week. As your first night approaches, you will want to get off to the best start with your new sleeping arrangements. In the next chapter we will look at why puppies cry, and how you can make sure *your* puppy is settled into a peaceful night-time routine with a minimum of fuss.

 SUMMARY

- Show children how to hold and cuddle the puppy gently.
- Feed your cat away from the puppy, and give the cat an escape route.
- Observe the rules of engagement between your puppy and your older dog.
- Supervise the puppy and make sure your older dog has his own space.
- Use food to give his crate the feel-good factor.

12

Silent nights

N ew puppy owners are not always aware that small puppies may need attention and cry during the night. 'It's worse than having a baby!' is a common observation. Whilst you didn't have to take your newborn baby into the garden at three in the morning, an outdoor vigil by torchlight is part and parcel of new-puppy ownership for most families. Night waking in puppies is usually confined to the first week or two, which is fortunate, because no matter how short-lived *your* nightly excursions may be, sleep deprivation is always horrible and can soon take some of the pleasure out of caring for a puppy.

During the day, it is a fairly simple matter to keep your puppy happy and occupied while he adjusts to his new home. At night-time, everything changes. The house becomes quiet; the grown-ups disappear into their beds. Mum, brothers and sisters are nowhere to be seen, and there is no familiar place of safety where he can curl up and hide until the grown-ups return.

Why puppies cry

People are often surprised to learn that many dogs are not naturally noisy. A dog's natural instinct is to communicate first through body language rather than through barking or whining. Yet many dogs have learned to make their views known through an extensive repertoire of sounds, long before their first birthday.

We can divide crying into two broad categories:

- **Fear or discomfort crying**
- **Learned crying**

Whilst many puppies quickly learn to make a noise in order to manipulate their owners, when a puppy first arrives in your home, the most likely cause of crying is fear. Small puppies are vulnerable and your puppy has inherited some behaviours that were once needed to protect his wild ancestors when they were puppies. A wolf cub left alone for long outside would soon become someone else's dinner. It is therefore vital for his survival that he is never unattended unless left in the safety of his den. If for any reason he becomes separated from his family, he will need to raise the alarm. On the other hand, it is important that he doesn't attract attention to the den itself. So whenever he is left inside it, remaining quiet is a good policy.

Many small puppies today still behave in a similar way. If at any time a small puppy is left alone *outside* of the place he considers to be his den, he will make a loud and alarming noise to alert his grown-ups to his predicament. He is saying, 'Help, I've been abandoned, rescue me NOW.' These are automatic and instinctive responses, and this is not something that your puppy can control. Inside the den, within reason, he will wait patiently and quietly for his grown-ups to return. Unfortunately, for the next few days, your puppy may not yet recognise the den you have made for him as a place of safety. This means that if you leave him alone, he will probably cry.

He has never had to sleep alone before.

The sheer volume of sound produced by this angelic bundle may astound you. Once a puppy is distressed, his cries become increasingly desperate and will tug mercilessly at your heartstrings. We humans seem to be programmed to respond to a puppy's distress signal just as his natural parents are, and resisting it is very difficult and upsetting. In addition to being stressful at any time of day, night-time crying causes sleep deprivation, which makes for clumsy and irritable puppy owners. Sleep deprivation can be a significant cause of domestic conflict as sleep-fuddled family members try to agree on the best course of action. However prepared you are, the howling *will* upset you and you will want it to stop as soon as possible.

🐾 Learning to be alone

You may have heard that learning to be alone is an important part of a new puppy's education. And this is absolutely true. All puppies need to learn to cope with being alone for short periods of time before they are three months old. This helps to ensure that the puppy will not suffer from separation anxiety later on in life. However, these first few nights alone are a somewhat unnatural situation for a puppy, simply because he has no familiar bed to rest in and feel safe.

In the long run, most people will want their puppy to sleep downstairs in his crate in the kitchen or utility room. And this is a good idea. But should you start as you mean to go on? Or should you make an exception for those first few nights when your puppy is feeling homesick?

There are two ways to approach this.

- Method 1: cold turkey
- Method 2: temporary room mates

Cold turkey

This is the harden-your-heart approach, and it involves putting the puppy to bed and leaving him to cry, right from the very first night. Most puppies will not want to be left alone at bedtime, but most will settle and sleep through the night without a problem within three or four nights. The vast majority of puppies settle within the week, and some will settle down to sleep on the first night without ever making a fuss.

If you have an older dog, this method works very well. Simply place the puppy in his crate in the same room as his new friend. He will be able to smell and hear

Getting your puppy to sleep through the night will be a priority.

If you have an older dog, your puppy will probably be happy downstairs from the start.

the other dog and this will make him feel safe. Most puppies will not cry at all in this situation.

However, if this is your first and only dog, there can be problems with the cold-turkey method. Your puppy may scream very loudly indeed when you leave him, or he may start screaming some time afterwards. If you have close neighbours, this could be a problem. The screaming will probably upset you far more than you think, and in a small house it may keep family members awake. You will need to decide in advance what you will do if this happens. Remember that puppies learn through the consequences of their behaviour. So it is not a good idea to open a crate door, or even to enter the room he is in, while the puppy is yelling. You will need to wait for a pause or break in his cries before attending to him.

With a very upset puppy that cries for much of the night, it can be difficult to tell whether he is yelling for company, or because he needs to relieve himself. Some puppies get so upset they empty their bowels in the crate and get themselves in a terrible mess, and shampooing a smelly wriggling puppy at 3 a.m. is not much fun.

Many new puppy owners do use the cold-turkey method without any problems, and without the puppy becoming too distressed, but it is important to recognise that, with some puppies, this is not an easy option. There is, however, another way, and one that many people find very successful.

Temporary room mates

This is a gentler introduction to being in your home. It involves placing your puppy in a sturdy, deep-sided box right next to your bed, where he can hear you and smell you. Many puppies will not cry at all if you do this. They feel safe and will settle down to sleep. You will probably wake when your puppy stirs in the night, and can let him out for a wee without disturbing the rest of the family. If you use his crate for this purpose, you will need to bring it downstairs with you in the morning.

The transition to sleeping in his own crate in the kitchen is made after four or five nights. At this point, the puppy has begun to accept his new den downstairs as a place of safety and crying is likely to be minimal. If he does cry, he will be far less distressed than a very homesick puppy on his first night.

The disadvantages of this second option are that some puppies don't settle next to your bed, and will cry anyway. You then stand even less chance of sleeping than you would have had with your puppy yelling in another room. Some people find it difficult to sleep with a puppy snuffling and snoring next to them, and if the puppy spends *too many* nights in your room, he may protest very loudly when he is finally moved downstairs. In this case, at least you have the reassurance of knowing that by this time your puppy is at ease in your home and will not feel completely abandoned.

The choice of method is yours. Temporary room mates may be the best option for family that does not have an older dog. But if you really don't like the idea of having a puppy in your room for a few nights, don't worry about using the cold-turkey approach. Most puppies will stop crying within three or four nights, and although it seems harsh, puppies don't seem to suffer any ill effects from this brief upset.

Getting ready for bed

Whichever method you use, you will probably need to get up in the night to let the puppy empty his bladder. We'll look at this in more detail in the chapter on house-training, but many puppies of eight weeks cannot last six or seven hours without a wee.

In order to give yourself the longest stretch of sleep, you will need to take your puppy out last thing at night, just before you go to bed. Decide in advance what time that will be and make sure that the puppy is given no food at all in the three or four hours before bedtime. That includes treats. Then, when you take him outside last thing at night, give him plenty of time to empty himself.

Puppies don't need water at night, provided they have not recently eaten a meal. And you should take his water away a good hour before bedtime, so that he doesn't tank himself up with liquid just before you shut him in. Have your torch and something warm to wear close to hand. And have some clean vetbed ready in case the puppy has already wet himself when you go in to him. Once you have put your puppy to bed, say good night and don't communicate with him any further. He will soon learn that people are boring at night-time and only play or chat during the day.

Set your alarm for about three to four hours after your puppy's last trip to his toilet area. This alarm gives you a chance to take the puppy out before his full bladder wakes him and he starts to cry. Pre-empting the puppy's need to go out is helpful because it avoids the puppy learning that crying gets him attention. If he wakes and cries before your alarm goes off, set your alarm a little earlier the following night. If he is fast asleep when you go in to him, you can set your alarm a little later the following night.

Many puppies are sleeping well within a week or two.

Night-time toilet trips

Carry your puppy from his crate to his toilet area. If you let him walk, he will get all wakeful and playful and will be less likely to settle back down again. As soon as he has done a wee, take him back to his crate and leave him. Keep any lighting to a minimum and don't chat to the puppy. No extra hugs and cuddles, just out and back in again. The point is to make this night-time trip very brief and unrewarding. If you make the whole thing a jolly jaunt, *he* will want to make it a regular arrangement.

Your individual puppy

No one can predict how your new puppy will behave at night. A fair proportion of puppies are simply angelic and barely cry at all. If your puppy is a screamer, it can come as quite a shock. Night-time excursions are not much fun, but these early problems will soon be a distant memory and silent nights will prevail once more in your home.

Whilst getting a puppy to be dry and quiet and to sleep at night is usually a fairly brief endeavour, house-training a puppy so that he is reliably clean during his waking hours takes a little longer. Puppies have short attention spans and poor bladder control, and you will be kept fairly busy for the next few weeks making sure that he empties himself in the right place. The next chapter is aimed at helping you make swift progress with house-training, so let's move on now and look at encouraging your puppy to be clean and dry at all times.

> ### SUMMARY
> - Don't release your puppy from the crate while he is crying.
> - Consider having your puppy sleep by your bed for the first few nights.
> - Restrict him to a small, washable area until he is able to keep that clean and dry.
> - Don't feed your puppy for four hours before your bedtime.
> - Try to take your puppy out during the night before nature calls and he cries.

13

Clean and dry

When I was small, our new puppies spent the first few nights by my mother's bed and were then moved into the kitchen. The entire family would spend the next few weeks following the puppy around and hopefully scooping him up just before he made a puddle. Accidents were frequent at first and puppies were scolded for them. At night, the kitchen floor would be smothered in newspaper. The puppy would empty himself on the floor and any newspaper he had not shredded would be cleared up in the morning.

House-training was often quite a prolonged process. The area covered with newspaper would be decreased over several weeks and eventually moved (weather permitting) to just outside the kitchen door. Paper-trained puppies often have a tendency to make what they consider good use of newspapers that they find for some months to come. This used to make for some interesting conversations. Some people still paper-train their puppies this way, but for most of us, crates have revolutionised house-training.

At eight weeks old, many puppies have very poor bladder control.

The modern approach

Every puppy instinctively wants to keep his home den clean, so we can use the crate to stretch out the gaps between bathroom breaks, and to avoid accidents. I'll give you some examples of house-training routines that do just this in a moment.

If you don't go out with your puppy, he'll just wait by the door to come in.

Of course, in order for any animal to be able to control where it empties itself, it needs more than just an ability to learn. It also needs the capability to hold on to the contents of its bladder and bowels. We therefore need to be sensitive to the physical maturity of the puppy as we work through this process.

Puppies have very little control over their bladders at eight weeks old. When they need to go, they need to go now! Little by little your puppy's ability to hold on for a bit longer will grow. Whilst you cannot influence the speed with which he develops a greater bladder awareness and capacity, you can influence your puppy's desire to use the new toilet area, and reduce his desire to toilet indoors. This is where crates come in handy.

Puppies love to wee where they have wee'd before, and hate to wee in their dens. The strategic and careful use of crate time in house-training helps to prevent accidents indoors, which in turn reduces your puppy's inclination to wee indoors in the future. He will try hard not to wee in his crate, so short periods of crate time encourage him to hold on, and his bladder will gradually be able to hold more urine for longer periods of time. Let's see how this works in practice.

Stage one 8–9 weeks: establishing a toilet area

This initial stage in toilet training is to help your puppy to get to know the new toilet area and to recognise it as a good place to relieve himself. During this stage you need to take full responsibility for making sure you place your puppy in his toilet area outdoors many times each day. It is a good idea to carry your puppy from his crate through the house and to put him down only when you reach the appropriate area. If you let him walk from his crate to the back door, at this point his control is so poor he is likely to have an accident on the way. Wait outside with the puppy for five minutes to give him plenty of chance to answer the call of nature.

In a busy family, it is quite a good idea to set an alarm to remind you to take him out half an hour after the last successful trip. Repeat throughout the day.

If the puppy fails to relieve himself on any of your outings to the garden, you need to crate him or supervise him *extremely* closely for ten to fifteen minutes and then try again. Supervise closely means literally not taking your eyes off the puppy for a second, preferably holding him on your lap or in your arms.

IMPORTANT NOTE: If your puppy cries when you place him in his crate, wait until he stops crying before you open the door to let him out. If you feel that crying in the crate is increasing, work through the procedures described in Chapter 21, 'The noisy puppy'.

When your puppy is outside the crate, confine him to a small area of washable floor. A single room, such as your kitchen, is ideal. When you put the puppy to bed at night, set your alarm for four hours' time and take the puppy out into the garden for a wee. If all goes well, set your alarm a little later each night. Aim for six hours of sleep by the end of the week, but be prepared for it to take another week or two.

House-training routine for stage one
At least once during the night, on waking, after eating, or running about:

1. Carry the puppy outside to his toilet area.
2. Stay outside with the puppy until he relieves himself, or for at least five minutes.
3a. If successful, praise the puppy and make a big fuss of him.
3b. If unsuccessful, crate or cuddle the puppy for ten minutes, then repeat from step 1.
4. When successful, bring the puppy indoors and give him (with the exception of night-time) the freedom of your kitchen.
5. Set an alarm for thirty minutes' time.
6. After ten minutes or so, watch the puppy quite closely.
7. When the alarm goes off, repeat from step 1.

The objective is to avoid any accidents whatsoever in the house. This takes a bit of practice though, and the chances are that you will slip up once or twice. Small puppies will sometimes wee again, just fifteen minutes or so after the last wee. Whatever you do, don't attempt to reprimand the puppy.

Why is punishment not helpful?
Apart from the ethical considerations of punishing an animal for something it doesn't understand and has little control over, punishment in house-training is now known to have disadvantageous side effects.

Puppies cannot associate a punishment with their own behaviour unless the two occur together, so there is no point in punishing a puppy once the deed is done. Punishing a puppy while he is in the *process* of emptying himself on your carpet may seem like a good idea, but rather than teaching him that carpets are not toilets, it usually simply teaches the puppy that weeing in your presence is a hazardous occupation.

Having decided that you have an unreasonable aversion to his natural bodily functions, your puppy may well hold on as long as possible when you take him to his toilet area. This is not a helpful development. Punishment may also encourage him to hide when he wees indoors in the future. Generally speaking, it is easier to clean up a puddle in the middle of the floor than under the sofa. So forget any idea of punishment, and focus on getting the puppy to the right place at the right time. If, and probably when, he has an accident, make sure you clean up effectively.

Cleaning up accidents

Dogs are renowned for their amazing sense of smell, and this ability can work against you when you are trying to house-train your puppy. If you leave the slightest trace of urine on your floor, he will detect it, and be tempted to wee there in the future. Unfortunately, some household cleaners contain chemicals that are found in urine and can make things worse.

You can buy special sprays and cleaning fluids, designed for house-training, from most pet shops. Otherwise, use plenty of hot soapy water and ammonia-free cleaning fluids.

By the end of the first week, if your puppy is relieving himself happily on most of his trips to the garden, and you have had no accidents for a couple of days, you can move on to stage two.

Stage two 9–12 weeks: developing self-control

What we aim to help the puppy achieve in stage two is some better awareness of his bladder and bowels, and some motivation to get to his toilet area when they need emptying. By the end of stage two, if you leave the back door open, in good weather, many puppies will be able and willing to take themselves outside to the toilet. If you leave the door shut, the puppy may wait by it for a moment before weeing on the floor. Your job is to continue to supervise closely when he is out of the crate, and to help him get to his toilet area at regular intervals.

Early on in stage two, many puppies will be able to last a six-hour stretch at night, say from midnight to 6 a.m. You can continue to stretch out the gap by setting your alarm fifteen minutes later each night, until you have a seven-hour gap. If the puppy wets his bed, put it in the washing machine on a hot wash and clean the crate thoroughly, then go back to setting your alarm half an hour *earlier* and increase the gaps with more caution.

Some puppies will last even longer. Provided there are no accidents, you can also stretch out the gaps between toilet trips during the day. Work your way from thirty minutes to forty-five minutes and so on. Some puppies may be able to last an hour or more between trips at three months old. Some will not cope with this reliably until they are four or five months old. You have to be guided by your puppy. If he is having accidents, shorten the gaps between toilet breaks.

During this stage, you can introduce a cue word, which your puppy will associate with doing a wee or a poo. Pick a word or short phrase (I use 'hurry up') and say it quietly as your puppy is emptying himself. Later on, you will be able to use the word to encourage him to empty himself at a time that is convenient to you, but don't attempt to do this yet. If you use the word and he does not oblige, you will have taught him that the word has no meaning.

Any ability to hold on is still relatively fragile, and a puppy under three months old is easily distracted. He won't remember that he needed to go out for a wee when there is anything interesting going on around him, and accidents are highly likely unless he is closely supervised. However for fifteen to twenty minutes after your puppy has emptied himself, you can relax a little as he will become increasingly unlikely to have an accident in this timeframe. When twenty minutes have passed after his last wee, you need to begin to keep an eye on the puppy for signs that he needs to go out. If you cannot do this, pop him in his crate for a few minutes, until it is time to go out again.

Key points for stage two

- Increase the night's sleep by fifteen minutes every few nights up to a seven-hour stretch.
- Continue to take the puppy out after waking, eating, playing and when there has been a gap since the last toilet break.
- Increase the length of the gap between breaks up to an hour.

If the puppy has been outside unsupervised and you don't know how long it is since he last did a wee, pop him in his crate for twenty minutes and then take him outside and supervise him. Repeat until he wees, then you can relax around him indoors for a while.

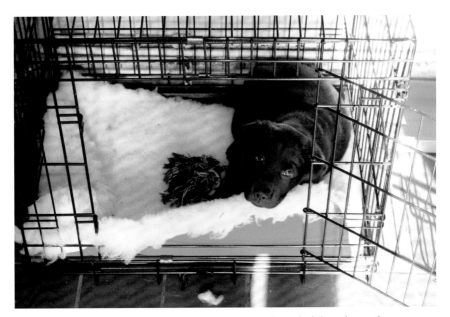

Your puppy won't wee in her crate if it is small enough and you don't leave her too long.

Simple house-training routine for stage two

On waking, after eating, or running about:

1. Walk with the puppy outside to his toilet area. He should be able to make it without an accident by now.
2. Preferably stay with the puppy until he relieves himself, or for at least five minutes.
3a. If successful, praise the puppy and make a big fuss of him.
3b. If unsuccessful in the toilet area, crate the puppy for twenty minutes then repeat from step 1.
4. As the puppy relieves himself, say 'hurry up' (or choose another phrase or word) in a soft and friendly way.
5. Bring him indoors and give him the freedom of your kitchen.
6. Set an alarm for forty-five minutes' time.
7. After the first twenty minutes, watch the puppy more closely or crate him for a few minutes.
8. When the alarm goes off, repeat from step 1.

Once your puppy can last about an hour between toilet breaks during the day, and has had no accidents for a few days, you are ready to begin to extend the clean zone in your house.

Stage three 3–6 months: extending the clean zone

By time they are three months old, many puppies are able to be clean and dry in a restricted area of your house. Extending this area is a gradual process, and it's important to remember that your puppy's memory and attention span are still very immature. If your puppy gets too far from the back door, he will relieve himself in the house.

Carpets are much more attractive to a puppy with a full bladder than a washable floor. Extend the clean zone to other rooms with washable floors before you include rooms with carpets. Introduce the puppy to carpets with caution and a lot of supervision. Initially, it is best to allow access to carpets only when the puppy has just emptied himself outdoors, and for no more than twenty minutes after that time. After twenty minutes, it is best to return him to the kitchen. Try not to rush this. The more often the puppy plays on your carpets *without* an accident, the less likely he will be to have an accident in the future. You are building good habits here and it is worth taking it slowly.

During stage three, you will also be able to extend the gaps between toilet breaks and by about six months of age, many puppies can last two to three hours without a wee.

Coping with setbacks

Many puppies will go through setbacks during house-training. Accidents may start occurring again just as you thought you were done with the whole process. The cause of the setback is often simply that we have stretched out the gaps between toilet breaks a little too quickly. Accidents are also quite common when a period of bad weather follows a nice dry spell. This is because the puppy has got used to emptying himself outdoors in comfort and does not appreciate being rained on or getting cold feet. This may mean returning to waiting outside with him until he does a wee, and shortening the intervals between toilet breaks for a while.

A puppy that is wetting himself frequently for no apparent reason, after previously being clean, may have a bladder infection and needs to be checked by the vet. Try to get a sample of his urine to take with you, as this will help the vet confirm his diagnosis.

Take it slowly

Make the house-training process easy on yourself. Progress in stages and don't move on until you have mastered the previous one. If you have slip-ups or setbacks, just drop back a stage and move on again a little more slowly.

Puppies like to sniff around for a bit before they do a wee.

Don't forget those key times when puppies are most likely to need a wee:

- **After waking**
- **After playing**
- **After eating**
- **Whenever it is has been a fair while since the last toilet break**

Bear in mind that giving a new puppy the free run of your home can be a recipe for house-training problems. Keep him in a small washable area until he can cope with keeping that clean and dry, and use the crate to help stretch out gaps between toilet breaks. Introduce access to carpeted parts of the house gradually and with care, and before you know it, your puppy will be clean and dry.

As if you didn't have enough to do, for the next few weeks you are going to need to get out and about with your puppy as much as you possibly can. Don't worry, you will be busy, but it will be fun! In the next chapter, we are going to look at the all-important process of socialising your dog.

 SUMMARY

- Use your puppy's den to increase gaps between toilet breaks.
- Take house-training slowly and in stages.
- Don't punish accidents – it's counter-productive.
- Introduce him to carpeted areas carefully and slowly.

14

Out and about

During the next few weeks, you will need to expose your puppy to as many new and interesting experiences as you can, and there are lots of ideas in this chapter to get you started on your excursions. Knowing that your actions over the coming weeks may have a profound influence on your puppy's future temperament and behaviour can feel a little daunting. If at any point you feel a little fed up with the effort involved, do consider how much you will enjoy the fruits of your labour. No dog can be truly happy if he is fearful or worried all the time, and the socialisation process that you are about to embark upon will help your dog grow up to be confident, brave and contented.

If your puppy finds any of these new experiences scary, and he might well do, your job is to think of a way to re-introduce that experience at a level, or in a way, that is not frightening. This can often be achieved simply by putting some distance between the puppy and the scary thing. A smelly and clanking dustbin lorry, for example, is a lot less frightening to a puppy at fifty yards than it is when you are standing just a few feet away.

Let's take a look to begin with at the kinds of experience you need to engineer for your pup.

Categories of experience

I find it helpful to divide socialisation experiences into four broad categories.

- People
- Machinery
- Animals
- Locations

He may need a little reassurance to begin with.

Machines are everywhere.

Our first and most important category is people. It is very easy, even in a normal lively family environment, to leave holes in your socialisation process. And nowhere is this more evident or more important than in socialising a dog with people. One problem is that at different times in our lives, we tend to mix with different groups of people. Some homes are relatively child-free zones, others have no men, some have teenagers but no small children. Many families have little or no contact with elderly or disabled people.

City puppies grow up with very different experiences from country puppies. You can see that it is quite possible for a four-month-old puppy never to have met a man, seen a train, met a toddler or a person in a wheelchair, or seen a horse or a sheep. We need to bear in mind that at four months, the window of socialisation is virtually closed and we do need to make an effort to make sure our puppies meet as many different kinds of people as possible before this point. Learning to accept new things later in life is a prolonged and laborious process.

We live in a very mechanised world. From the cars and lorries outside in the street to the vacuum cleaners and hairdryers we use indoors, and not forgetting the leaf blowers and pressure washers we use in the garden, machines are everywhere. Your dog needs to be comfortable with this. Getting along with other animals is also a part of life, and you need to make an effort to help your puppy meet plenty of friendly dogs and cats, and even to feel relaxed around larger animals, such as horses and cattle.

The things people do to dogs

Part of socialisation is accustoming a puppy not only to different types of people, but also to the different things that people do to dogs. Not everyone is aware of how dogs like to meet and greet. Strangers may thrust their hands and even their faces against your dog's mouth, vets will want to examine his body and even look down his throat. A kindly passer-by may grab at his collar if he wanders out through the gate left open by a careless visitor. Children may take toys from his mouth, and friends may ruffle his fur the wrong way and even hug or cuddle him. He must bear all these things with equanimity and a good grace.

Daily grooming sessions will help your puppy adjust to being poked, prodded and generally handled. But he must also be easily restrained. Don't be tempted to place your puppy on the ground each time he wriggles or struggles in your arms. If you do this, he will quickly learn to squirm each time he wants to get down. Hold him firmly until he relaxes and *then* release him. Adult dogs are not natural cuddlers. Make sure you get *your* small puppy used to being cuddled and that you handle his feet, ears and mouth on a regular basis. Then it will not seem shocking to him when a vet or stranger grips or examines him.

Polite puppies are happy to be examined by strangers.

Of all the things that people do to dogs, there is no human behaviour quite so strange, to a puppy, as that exhibited by many children. And you will need to make socialisation with children one of your top priorities.

Make children a priority

Meeting children can be a real effort if you don't have any. It can become something that you keep putting off, and before you know it, you have a six-month-old puppy that growls at your neighbour's toddler. Even if you have your own children at home, you are going to have to make an effort to introduce your puppy to other people's offspring. Getting comfortable around children under four is especially important.

Very small children are unpredictable. They move differently and sound different from other people. Your dog needs to be comfortable with this. We discussed in Part One how the roots of aggression lie in fear. Your dog needs to feel safe around children of all shapes and sizes so that they can be safe around him. The consequences of failure don't bear thinking about. We'll have a look in a moment, at some great places to meet kids.

Preparing for outings

Even if it were possible, you cannot simply bring all these experiences that your puppy needs into his home or garden. He also needs to experience different types of weather and terrain. He needs to feel as comfortable in the town centre as he does in your garden. You have no option but to get out and about with your puppy. Fortunately, there are a number of locations that will enable you to introduce him to different environments and to meet a wide range of people.

When you go out with your puppy, always take a small bag of puppy food, so that if he is at all timid or shy, you can give approaching strangers a little piece of food to feed him with. You may normally avoid visiting busy places and try to shop during quiet times, but for the next few weeks you are going to have to reverse that policy because lots of people is just what your puppy needs.

If you are shy, this won't be easy for you, but it has to be done. Remember to smile as people come towards you – they are then more likely to stop and talk to your puppy. If it isn't possible for you to make all these trips personally, it's okay to get some help. Your puppy doesn't need you to be there every time; he just needs a sympathetic, familiar and understanding person who will help him enjoy meeting new people.

You are probably going to be doing quite a bit of driving for the next few weeks and this is a good thing. Puppies that do not experience much car travel when small may suffer badly from motion sickness later on. Don't worry if your puppy is carsick on the first few outings, this will pass, especially if you are able to make lots of short journeys with him to help him adjust.

What about disease?

During the time period before your puppy's immunity has taken full effect, you may be worried about your puppy being exposed to disease. We have looked at this in some detail in Part One. The compromise that most puppy owners adopt is to carry the puppy around until he is fully protected by his vaccinations. Putting the dog in a large shoulder bag like the one pictured opposite can be a great solution.

No one can tell you what you should do with your puppy, and with some very large-breed dogs, taking them everywhere in your arms, or even in a bag, is impractical if not impossible. You may feel that you must take the risk and place the dog on the ground before the vaccination process is complete. In this case, it is important to avoid ground that is highly likely to be contaminated. This will include any areas that are popular with local dog walkers.

Once the puppy is fully immune, you can take him anywhere and put him down on the ground. This opens up a whole new world for him, as things undoubtedly look different from down there.

Suggestions for outings

Time is short and it is a good idea to fit in at least two or three outings each week (one of these will be his first visit to your vet). I have listed a few suggestions. You will need to use some of these ideas more than once or come up with ideas of your own.

A shoulder bag will keep your puppy off the ground.

The supermarket Save this trip for fine weather. Don't go when it is raining because you are not going to take the puppy inside; you are going to stand outside the main door with the puppy in your arms, and wait for people to approach you. Puppies are magnets, especially for children, and it won't be long before you have drawn quite a crowd. Make sure you go outside of school hours so that you get to meet school-age children, too.

The pet shop Check whether your local large pet shop allows dogs to go inside. Most do. Visit the shop on a Saturday when it is busy. You will find plenty of children and their parents near the small-animal displays and may get to meet other puppies and friendly older dogs, too. Ask the owners if they have been vaccinated or keep the puppy well out of their reach.

Obviously, men especially have to use some common sense when talking to other people's children. Make sure that the parents are aware and happy that their kids are talking to you and stroking your dog. You don't want to end up in a fight, or being accused of grooming something other than your dog! Nowhere is this more important than outside the school gates.

The school gates Standing outside a school at the end of the school day is a great way to meet heaps of children. If you don't have school-age kids or grandchildren, try to find a parent who will let you accompany them when they collect their own children. Again, being accompanied is probably more important for men.

The local pub If you have one of these that welcomes dogs, this is a great place for your puppy to meet new people. Remember to keep him up on your lap until his vaccinations are complete.

The village pub is a great place to meet people.

A visit to the railway station will help your puppy meet people and machines.

The railway station If you go at the right time, your local railway station is a good way to combine meeting people and machinery. Make sure you go at around six in the evening on a working day and meet the commuters coming off the train.

The bus ride For many of us who have grown up in rural areas, a bus ride is a bit of a novelty. It is, however, a great way to get a puppy up close and personal to a large machine, and lots of lovely people. Take a short ride at a fairly busy time of day and you can guarantee lots of admirers for your puppy.

The town centre A busy town centre on a Saturday morning is another great way to meet people of all shapes and sizes, and to see a substantial amount of traffic. This is especially important for a rural puppy, who may be quite intimidated by cars rushing past him.

A friend's house Visiting a friend or neighbour who owns a friendly, vaccinated dog can be a good experience for your puppy, provided you are willing to supervise and to cut the visit short if it is not going well. Meeting and playing with other dogs is important, but you need to be careful. Even the nicest dogs don't always welcome young puppies and a bad experience at this age can actually make your puppy afraid of other dogs.

Your checklist

Make a checklist of experiences for your puppy and stick it up on your fridge. Each time you complete one of the targets, put a tick in the relevant box. As you can see, some of the outings listed above will kill a lot of birds with one stone. In the town centre you will see cars and pushchairs, buses and motorbikes, and people of all shapes and sizes. You may even find people in uniforms or hats.

Take every opportunity that comes your way to show your puppy something new. When you hear the dustbin lorry coming down the road, grab your puppy and carry him out to watch. Encourage the bin men to stroke him if they want to. If there is a street market or a brass band in town, go along. In the summer, fêtes, markets, country shows and carnivals are great ways to see all sorts of unusual sights – people on stilts, wearing costumes, carrying balloons and so on. Grab any seasonal opportunities that come your way and take every chance you can to include your puppy in family visits and outings.

🐾 Down on the ground

Each experience that you have arranged for your puppy needs to be repeated all over again when your puppy is fully immune and can be placed on the ground. Meeting people from ground level is very different from meeting people in the safety of a strong pair of arms, especially for very small dogs.

Once your puppy does not need to be carried, you can also introduce him to the joys of the countryside. Take him to a field where he can learn to explore muddy puddles. Take him to the beach and let him scamper over the sand and play in the shallows. Outdoors he can have fun watching leaves blow around in the wind and follow scent trails through the grass. Much of this exploration will consist of you sitting on the ground waiting patiently, or walking about randomly in different directions. We'll look at exercise and training later on, but the important thing is to recognise that at three or four months old your puppy doesn't need long walks of any kind, he just needs these new experiences.

Splashing in the shallows is all part of the fun.

Restraining your puppy

For these early outings, there will be some locations where your puppy needs to be restrained for his own safety. If you are not careful this need for restraint can cause problems in later training. One of the most common problems that

The harness may feel a little strange a first.

owners of medium and large dogs struggle with is pulling on the lead. While you are out and about, socialising your puppy, it is natural that he will sometimes tug and pull towards things that interest him. Later on, you will train him to walk nicely at your side, but at this stage, simply avoiding an association between pulling and wearing a collar and lead will help you with lead training later.

Rather than having your puppy wear a collar and lead when you take him into town, consider using a harness. This serves a number of purposes. A properly fitted harness is virtually impossible for the puppy to slip out of and is therefore safer. A harness where the lead attaches at the front reduces pulling, and any harness will prevent the puppy getting into a habit of leaning into his collar.

Attach the lead to your puppy only when you need to for his own safety; a small puppy does not necessarily need to be restrained in the countryside, where there are no hazards, as he will instinctively follow you. We'll talk about this in more detail when we look at the puppy recall.

What about puppy classes?

Some people take their puppies to a puppy socialisation class. This can work brilliantly, but there are risks. A badly run puppy class with inadequate supervision may allow some puppies to be bullied by more forceful personalities, or may encourage yapping and whining. Many puppies will benefit from a well-run class where there is a good level of supervision and few enough students for each to be given sufficient attention from the instructor. Try to get recommendations from local people or your vet, and go along for a session without your puppy first, to see if you are happy with the way the class is run. If you have plenty of friends with nice friendly dogs, you don't need to attend a class if you don't want to.

Keeping it up

When you have completed your checklist of targets, you will have a very confident and friendly three or four month old. This is a great reward for all the effort you have put in, but before you hang up your coat and put the final tick on your chart, I do need to let you know that you haven't quite finished yet.

It is entirely possible to take this friendly, confident puppy, shut him away for a few months and end up with a fearful dog at the end of it. The socialisation process needs to continue, albeit at a gentler pace now, for much of your puppy's first year. Don't panic, it won't be the frantic scramble for new experiences that you may feel you have just survived. But you will need to remember to include your puppy in outings and visits for at least the next few months so that he does not forget all that he has learned. If your puppy is very much part of family life and goes everywhere with you, this will happen naturally. But if you are fairly reclusive or live quite a quiet life, you will need to make a special effort to get out and about.

Getting out and about on four legs

For many puppy owners, the moment at which the puppy's vaccinations are complete is an exciting one. At last the puppy can join in the family's activities without worrying about infection, your back can have a rest from carrying your rapidly growing friend, and the puppy can run around and enjoy himself in the countryside.

This often raises concerns of a different nature. What if your puppy runs away? And how can you teach him to come when you call him? We look at these questions in our next chapter.

SUMMARY
- Make sure your puppy has met all sorts of people before he is four months old.
- Make meeting children a priority.
- Carry your puppy on outings before his immunity kicks in.
- Take puppy food with you so that strangers can feed him.
- At four months old, your puppy needs new experiences more than long walks.

15

Beginning the puppy recall

Watching someone try to catch a puppy can be quite entertaining. Puppies are as slippery as eels, can turn on a sixpence and love being chased. Four legs definitely have the advantage over two, and your chances of catching your puppy diminish with every passing day. Chasing him also teaches him to run *away* from you rather than *towards* you, which is never a good idea. So unless you are a talented athlete, or enjoy making a spectacle of yourself, I strongly recommend you teach your puppy to come when he is called!

This chapter is not about training your puppy to be obedient. It is about grasping a unique opportunity that presents itself at this specific stage in a puppy's life, to lay foundations for obedience training, which comes later. What we are going to do with this opportunity is build a strong association in your puppy's mind between the sound of your recall command and the act of running towards you.

A unique opportunity

One of the saddest things I ever hear is the owner of a six-month-old dog asking, 'When can I let my puppy off the lead?' The truth is that the owner has missed a wonderful opportunity. In Chapter 4, 'Influencing growth and development', we talked about your puppy's natural safety response to being placed on the ground. For the first few weeks after you bring him home, your new friend will want nothing more in the world than to be next to you. Put him down on the ground and walk briskly away and he will trot after you as though you are giving off some kind of irresistible force of attraction!

This glorious state of affairs is a temporary one, and the safety response disappears over the next couple of months. As your dog grows in independence and the wide world beckons, he will want to follow in your footsteps about as much as a teenage boy wants to hang out with his mum and dad at weekends.

It is important, therefore, not to be tempted to delay this training, even though there is a lot going on at the moment. Now is simply the right time to get that puppy off a lead and to start laying the foundations of a good recall.

Your recall signal

You are going to be teaching your puppy to recall to a signal. This can be a word such as 'here' or 'come' or it can be a few pips on a whistle. I recommend the whistle because it gives you more control over who uses this most important of commands.

There are two parts to this early puppy recall training. The first stage is the part where you deliberately create lots of situations in which the puppy runs towards you and is rewarded. This makes running towards you deeply pleasurable for the puppy. The second stage is to associate your recall signal with this pleasurable act.

Take every opportunity to encourage your puppy to run after you.

Important information

The signals we use to cue different behaviours in our dogs are easily poisoned. What does that mean? Well, we teach our dogs the meaning of different signals or commands by pairing those signals with an action. A well-trained dog sits when he is told to sit and comes when he is told to come because he has built up an association in his brain between the signal and the action with which we want him to respond. A poisoned signal is one that the dog has associated with an inappropriate behaviour. For example, if your puppy hears you shouting 'come' while he is chasing a bee, or scratching his ear, the unique association of the word 'come' with the act of running towards you is broken. If this happens more than once, it will greatly diminish the power of the word 'come' when you try to use it as a command in the future. We call this a poisoned command.

Don't let this happen to *your* recall signal. To avoid poisoning your recall command, you will not use it AT ALL in stage one of recall training (below) and you will use it during stage two only when the puppy is actually in the act of moving towards you. Using a whistle will help you to protect your recall signal, because you can put the whistle away after training and keep it out of reach of your children.

Stage one in recall training

Remember, you will not be using any recall signal yet. This stage is about teaching the puppy that running fast towards a person is hugely rewarding. This is not difficult because puppies like chasing people, and because your small puppy will have a deep need to be near you. We can make it even more fun for him by giving him some extra attention and even a treat when he reaches your side. Your objective is to teach him that running after you is the best fun in the world.

Exercise one: getting your puppy to chase you

1. Place your puppy on the ground.
2. Sneak a few steps away, attract his attention with a squeaky noise if necessary, and walk farther away from him.
3. As he runs towards you, crouch down to his level.
4. When he reaches you, gather him into your arms and make the biggest fuss of him.

If at any point the puppy seems to be happy to let you walk away (this can

Make reaching you the best thing in the world.

happen if he feels very safe, perhaps in your garden), you can trigger his chase response. Make sure that there is no one else around for him to turn to. If there is someone with you, they must remain next to you. Move away from the puppy briskly, attract his attention with a squeaky noise and handclap, run if necessary, and *keep going*. He won't be able to resist.

Sometimes, when he reaches you, give him a juicy edible treat. This is especially important with a more confident puppy that is not too worried when you move away from him. Spend a couple of weeks of daily practice on this exercise.

Tips for daily practice

Put your puppy down on the ground at every opportunity and walk away from him. Encourage him to trot after you, attract his attention and keep changing direction. Allow the puppy to catch up with you often. Reward him generously with much fuss and attention when he does so. Give him a tasty food reward from time to time. Make reaching you, and being with you, the best thing in the world.

Avoiding mistakes

Avoid giving your puppy opportunities to practise moving *away* from you.

The worst thing you can do is follow your puppy around. This is what many people do when they take a puppy for a walk. Don't fall into this trap. Every time your puppy starts moving away from you, turn around and walk the other way. A very common mistake is for people to allow their children to chase the puppy. I cannot emphasise too strongly that you must never allow anyone to chase your puppy at *any time*. Puppies love being chased just as much as they love chasing people. Recall training is about teaching a puppy to run towards you. The very last thing you want him to do is run away from people.

Stage two in recall training

Once you have got your puppy running towards you each time you move away from him, you can begin to introduce the recall signal. I suggest you use a whistle right from the start. If you don't want to use a whistle, pick a verbal command, such as 'here' or 'come', and stick to it. You can train additional signals once the puppy is responding well to the first one.

Here is the important part again – you must give the recall signal *only when the puppy is already running towards you*! Do not under any circumstances be tempted to test the power of the whistle to induce your puppy to come. If it succeeds, you will be tempted to use the whistle again in more challenging circumstances. When it fails, and it will, you will have poisoned your recall. If you need to take your puppy home and he is playing or distracted, walk over to him calmly and pick him up, or get him to chase after you by running away from him. Be patient, we are building a wonderful habit here, there will be time for obedience later.

Exercise two: introducing your signal

Try to use the same tone of voice each time you call.

1. Put the puppy on the ground and put some space between you.
2. Move away from the puppy and, if necessary, attract his attention with a handclap or squeak.
3. Once he is rushing towards you, and just before he reaches you, give a single recall signal ('come' or pip pip pip on the whistle).
4. Reward the puppy generously when he arrives.

Don't be tempted to repeat your signal. You want your puppy to come to a single command. Associating multiple signals with any behaviour can quickly result in more and more commands being required before the dog will respond. You don't want to be the person standing at the edge of the field, empty lead in hand, endlessly blowing the whistle or shouting, 'Here, here, come here, HERE, COME HERE!' before your dog will even throw you a cursory glance.

Tips for daily practice

Try to practise several times a day. You can practise indoors, too. Wait until other members of the family are out of the way and put the whistle around your neck. Have some treats or some of your puppy's daily food allowance to hand. Every time he trots towards you, blow the whistle and feed him when he reaches you. The more you do this, the better.

Don't be tempted to test your recall whistle yet, by blowing it while your puppy is playing happily with a feather. Save it for when he is already running in your direction. What you are doing with the exercises in this chapter is laying the foundations that underpin a successful recall. When you have completed working on these exercises, you will have taught your puppy that the recall signal is a wonderful thing, and this will make training so much easier later on.

Of course, time spent with a puppy outdoors is not just about training. Part of the fun of having a puppy is the time you can spend playing together. So, whilst we will discover how to create a permanent and reliable recall response in the final chapter of this section, we need to take a look first at the important topics of exercise and play.

Don't blow the recall whistle whilst he is playing with his feather.

SUMMARY
- Never chase your puppy.
- Never give a recall signal unless your puppy is running towards you.
- Practise running *away* from your puppy every day.
- Recall your puppy often *while he runs towards you.*
- Reward him generously when he reaches you.

16

Exercise and play

Walking the dog each day is a wonderful tradition. It is also a chance to escape from the rush of modern life for an hour or so, to be alone with your thoughts, or to chat with a friend in the fresh air. The daily walk is one of the few activities busy people can engage in without guilt. Indeed, we can actually feel virtuous about striding out with the dog because we know it is good for both of us.

A daily walking routine is something that many new puppy owners look forward to with great enthusiasm, and for some it was a significant factor in their decision to bring a dog into their lives. Once your puppy has completed his course of vaccinations and you no longer have to carry him everywhere, you may be eager to set off on your first hike together. But before you grab your coat and wellies, let's have a look at just how much walking your new friend actually needs.

Daily exercise

In Part One we talked about the five-minute rule that is often quoted to new puppy owners – that is five minutes of exercise per day for every month of the puppy's age. This time limit does not include time that puppies spend simply playing by themselves in the garden, but refers to the more structured type of exercise that we humans organise for them, such as long walks and ball games.

This five-minute rule is a useful guideline for those who are unsure about just how much walking their puppy needs, and for those who might otherwise be tempted to walk their puppy for long distances. But it needs to be applied with common sense and it is probably not necessary to follow it too obsessively.

The study on puppy exercise that we discussed in Part One highlighted the risks of allowing puppies to clamber up and down steep steps. But it also

Ball games on the beach are a lot of fun.

showed that the puppies in the study that had been allowed access to off-lead exercise were at lower risk of joint problems than the other puppies, suggesting that exercise of the free-play variety is beneficial. This seems to support the common-sense view that puppies allowed to play and run around in the garden are not going to come to any harm.

In conclusion, it is sensible to limit your puppy's structured exercise carefully, but when it comes to free play, it's probably fine to use your judgement and step in if you think your puppy needs a rest. There is no point in allowing your puppy to be exhausted while playing with children or other dogs, but there is little evidence that play of this kind is actually harmful. On the other hand, it is a good idea to save the long hiking holidays you have been looking forward to until after your dog's first birthday.

Collie and pup playing with a tug toy.

Older puppies

For older puppies and adult dogs, some dog professionals recommend that extensive exercise is used as a management tool to keep the dog's energy levels within acceptable boundaries. The theory is that a tired dog will be easier to train and manage at home. This strategy is not as effective as you might think. Before you dig out your roller blades, bear in mind that dogs are descended from animals designed to hunt down caribou and other large prey. Many breeds of dog still have the capacity, once fit, to run many miles in a single day without stopping. Intensively exercising a healthy adult dog will create a very fit adult dog, and not much more. If you are training for a triathlon, you may enjoy the process. But trying to wear your dog out in order to control him is unlikely to be effective in the long term.

Dogs, like people, need exercise. Like people, it is possible to get a dog to a very high level of fitness, but most dogs will remain healthy without being pushed to the *limits* of their potential. And just like people, your dog won't suffer horribly if on one particular day, you cannot walk him. As a general rule, many medium to large dogs will do very well with an hour's walk at one end of the day, and thirty minutes or so at the other, especially if you spend some time throwing a ball or retrieving dummy for the dog at some point. If you have a large garden, you can fulfil a lot of your dog's exercise needs with retrieving games. Bear in mind also that some breeds of dog have special needs when it comes to exercise. Brachycephalic (flat-faced) dogs, for example, such as bulldogs and pugs, lack the ability to cool themselves effectively and need to be protected from intense exercise or from exercise in very warm conditions.

Exercise through play

Whilst adults may look forward to the prospects of long walks through the early morning dew with their new dog, children look forward to welcoming a new puppy into the home for very different reasons. Mostly they look forward to the prospect of playing with the puppy. Much of a small puppy's exercise needs are fulfilled simply through play, but a puppy's expectation of a game is very different from that of a child, and there is great scope here for confusion and upset. We'll have a closer look at this issue in a moment.

If you have an older dog, or a friend's dog, that is willing to play with your puppy, this can be very beneficial for him. He will be learning important dog communication skills in addition to getting a bit of a workout.

As the game goes on, some puppies will get more and more excited and appear to be quite hysterical, zooming around and crashing into things. Your presence here is important. Often the older dog will stop the game at this point. However, you may need to intervene and put a stop to the game to let the puppy calm down for a while. When the older dog has had enough, he will simply stand up, still and tall, and stop responding to the puppy to indicate that the game is over.

Brachycephalic dogs like this bulldog puppy need to be exercised with extra care.

Dog play is rough. It involves clashing teeth, a lot of noise and often includes bouts of chasing and barging. Both dogs know the rules, how to stop and start the game, and both are well protected by a thick layer of fur. You can see where this can all go badly wrong when children get involved.

Playing with children

I receive a lot of questions from parents who are very upset by the way their new puppy interacts with their children. The puppy seems to bite the children all the time, growl at them, tear their clothing and even draw blood. Every game seems to end in tears and with the puppy being told off. Many are concerned that the puppy has aggressive tendencies and are worried that they have brought a potentially dangerous dog into their home.

This situation arises because the children are triggering the kind of rough play that is normal for puppies and older dogs, and lack the ability to control the game or end it; nor are they able to judge when the puppy is becoming overexcited. Children love to roll on the ground, which puppies interpret as an invitation to rough play, and they tend to squeal a lot, which the puppy interprets as enthusiasm for the game. If the puppy bites another dog too hard, the other dog may snap a warning that your dog recognises as a clear signal to back off. Unfortunately, your child's cries of pain when the puppy bites too hard are not recognised by the puppy as indicating pain at all, and may only spur him on to more biting. As you can see, there is a bit of a language barrier here, and things can get very out of hand.

The solution to this problem is largely one of supervision. Older children can and should be taught to stand up and remain still when they want the game to end, but younger ones tend to simply panic and run around with the puppy chasing and nipping them. This means that you will need to be on hand to intervene. In the long run, it is best to discourage this kind of rough-and-tumble play between children and dogs, and to teach children to interact with the puppy in a more structured way, so that they can remain in control.

Structured play

If rough play of a free-for-all nature isn't such a great way to play with puppies, what should we do? Let's look again at some of the activities that puppies enjoy.

When we watch puppies play with other dogs, we can see that they enjoy:

- Chasing
- Being chased
- Tugging
- Barging
- Mouth wrestling

Some of these, mouth wrestling and barging for example, are obviously unsuitable. We talked in the last chapter about how chasing a puppy can interfere with recall, so that means being chased is out of the question. That leaves us with chasing and tugging. What can we do with those? Fortunately there is great potential for fun here, with both tugging and retrieving games.

Apart from the recall training exercises in the previous chapter, the best way to indulge a puppy's enjoyment of chasing games is to teach him to retrieve.

Many puppies have a natural instinct for retrieving.

Retrieving

Many puppies have a natural instinct for retrieving, that is to say, they are more than happy to chase after a ball and pick it up, and may even bring it back. Roll a ball a little way and see if your puppy will chase it. If he picks it up and returns to you, don't snatch it from him, but let him hold it for a while as you pet him and tell him how clever he is. You can encourage your puppy to return to you by throwing the ball down a narrow hallway, where he cannot skirt around you as he returns, or by sitting just in front of his bed, where he may instinctively want to take his prize.

Retrieving is actually quite a complex chain of behaviours and the instinct for chasing a moving object is very weak in some dogs, and vulnerable in many others. It is quite easy to put a dog off fetching your ball, possibly forever, by boring him witless with endless retrieves. The secret to keeping your dog chasing after the ball is to stop while he is still having fun.

It is traditional to throw sticks for dogs, but there have been many recorded instances of severe and even fatal throat injuries to dogs resulting from this game, so I recommend you use a ball or a safe alternative, such as the one in this illustration.

Sticks can be hazardous, but this is a safe alternative.

Fetching a ball or toy is just the start of retrieving. The retrieving game can be developed to challenge the cleverest dog, with hidden balls and longer and more difficult retrieves. You can even teach the dog to respond to hand signals and whistles at a distance.

Playing tug games

Most puppies will enjoy playing with a tug toy. You hold one end of a piece of thick rope, and the puppy holds the other. It is probably best not to do this with your dog if you want to get involved with gundog work, as there is a school of thought that it could interfere with his soft mouth. A great many puppies are extremely fond of tugging games and can be kept happy for long periods of time this way.

You will need to build some rules into your tug games, in order to ensure they do not get out of hand, and that you do not reward the dog for bad behaviour. Dogs should not be allowed to begin playing until you give the signal, saying the word 'tug' for example. And they must be taught to let go when you decide that the game is over. Jumping and snapping at the rope when you try to put it away is not acceptable, and dogs that become very overexcited or angry during a tug game should not be allowed to play. Playful growling with a wagging tail is fine.

You can teach a simple 'drop it' command using food. Have some tasty chicken or roast beef in a pocket or bag and hold a piece in front of the puppy's nose. As soon as he releases the tug toy say, 'Good,' and throw the treat well away from you. When he returns, tell him, 'Tug,' and offer him the rope again. When you are ready to finish the game, put the rope away while he is collecting a treat. Once he has got the hang of releasing the rope to collect his treat, you can add your cue words 'drop it' before you offer him the treat, and he will soon drop the rope on command.

Teaching tricks

A great way to get older children involved in playing with a puppy in a more structured way is to help them to teach him some tricks. If your children have no previous experience with dog training, tricks are an ideal way to start, because it doesn't matter if they get it wrong. Older children can easily teach a puppy to high five with a paw, to crawl through one of those play tunnels that lots of toddlers have, to stand with all four feet in a box, or to touch a brightly coloured target with his nose. You will need to teach them the five stages in training, which you can read about in Chapter 20, 'Towards obedience'. They gain as much from these games as the puppy does and it's a lot more fun than being bitten and jumped on.

Remaining in control

Playing with your puppy is a lot of fun provided that you remain in control. You need to decide when the game starts and when it stops, and your decision should be final. You should *keep possession* of important toys, such as your tug rope and your retrieving ball. That way they remain exciting and rewarding activities for the puppy. You can provide him with other toys to carry around or chew, but bear in mind he will usually either destroy or eat them, or lose them outside in the garden. It is the toys *you* control and produce for a special game that have real value, so keep them in a safe place where he cannot reach them. Remember to supervise children closely until they are old enough to control these games effectively.

Playing is a great opportunity for learning, and for building a bond between your puppy and other members of his family. It is also a time when behaviour can get out of control. The more excited the puppy gets, the rougher he becomes. Many new puppy owners are surprised, not only by the pain caused by their puppy's bites, but also by the ferocity with which they are delivered. Don't panic! Fierce behaviour in tiny puppies is actually quite normal. We'll have a closer look at coping with your little biter in the next chapter.

SUMMARY

- Supervise play with young children and teach older ones how to end the game.
- Reserve rough-and-tumble games for play between dogs.
- Structure retrieving and tug games.
- Stop the game while your puppy is still enjoying it.
- Encourage your children to teach the puppy tricks.
- Ensure you remain in control of your puppy's games.

17
Biting and growling

t can be quite a shock to discover just how fearsome puppies sound when they are playing. Before you rush off to have him certified, I want to reassure you that it is completely normal for your small puppy to growl *ferociously* as he plays. This is not a sign of aggression, simply a sign of his enthusiasm for the game and an indicator of his level of excitement. The more excited he gets, the noisier he may become.

If you begin to suspect that you have adopted a furry and determined croco-dile, you will not be alone. All puppies bite when they are playing. Some puppies bite so hard that they draw blood, and it is very common for new puppy owners to be concerned that something is wrong. Again, whilst unfortunate, this level of biting is not a sign of aggression. It is simply a part of being a healthy two- or three-month-old pup. The objective of this chapter is to reassure you that your puppy is behaving normally, and to show you how to teach your little crocodile to be gentle with his mouth.

Many puppies growl fiercely when they tug at your clothes.

Self-control

Let's look at an example. I feed my dogs, including puppies, on a raw diet, and my puppies are given whole, raw, chicken wings to eat. The largest bone in a chicken wing is about the thickness of the bones in my little finger. An eight-week-old Labrador puppy can crush one of these bones with a single bite, and pulverise the entire length of the bone in a few seconds. It is quite an eye opener to watch this for the first time.

My point is that even at eight weeks, this little dog has a seriously powerful bite capable of crushing a small prey animal in order to swallow it. But before you back away in horror from your own small furball, consider the fact that at eight weeks, a normal puppy has already learned *not to use this power* on his friends. If I put my little finger into an eight-week-old puppy's mouth, it may hurt quite a bit when he bites me, occasionally a puppy may even draw blood (though most puppies do not), but my finger remains intact. This little dog is *already* controlling the pressure he exerts with his jaws, depending on what is inside them. He is deliberately trying not to hurt me, despite appearances.

The fact that your puppy is able to refrain from crushing your fingers and mangling your flesh when he plays with you, when he undoubtedly has the ability to do so, is due to a process called bite inhibition. It is a process that began some weeks ago as he played in the nest with his brothers, sisters and mother. By the time you collect your puppy and take him home, he will already have learned to pull his punches. His mother will have taught him not to bite so hard that it hurts her. However, your puppy's mum has a nice fur coat to protect *her* skin and you do not. So you have a bit more work to do yet.

Practical stages in bite inhibition

It is tempting to try to stamp out puppy biting altogether, right from the beginning. However, most experts believe that it is important you do this in gradual stages rather than suddenly by punishing the puppy for biting. It is thought that if we prevent biting too *quickly*, the puppy may not learn what is appropriate pressure, and may not be capable of moderating the force of his bite in the future.

Teaching your puppy this kind of self-control takes a little time and patience, but the worst will be over in a few weeks. Your job is to extend the rules taught to your puppy by his mother, and to teach him how much pressure he can bring to bear on *human* skin, without causing pain.

Puppies bite very hard!

Withdrawing attention

At eight to nine weeks, your puppy will sometimes bite very hard, and at other times more gently. He is still learning how hard is *too* hard. Your job is to give him feedback and inform him in no uncertain terms when he has hurt you. Whenever your puppy hurts you with his teeth, give an 'ouch' and then terminate the game immediately. If the puppy was on your lap, put him on the floor. If you were sitting on the floor with him, stand up. Some puppies will back off immediately if you give a sharp squeal, others will attack you with renewed enthusiasm as they find the noise quite exciting. So you may need to experiment a little with the way in which you respond.

For some people, it is a great relief to discover that they do not have to play with the puppy when he is behaving like this. It is perfectly acceptable to end games that get too rough. Your puppy will not be emotionally harmed if you do not join in with his biting games, and over the space of the next few weeks he needs to learn not to bite at all.

Redirection

Whilst hurting you is not acceptable, puppies do have to have an outlet for their need to bite and chew. The answer is to redirect the biting onto an appropriate toy. So, as soon as you have ended the game, give your puppy a chew toy to bite on. A puppy that finds it very hard to calm down at this point can be placed quietly in a crate or playpen with his chew toy. The important thing is that he learns that hurting you causes an end to his fun game, and that chew toys are for biting, not fingers.

Persist in withdrawing your attention and in redirecting the puppy's harder bites onto his toys for the next few weeks and you will begin to see results. The puppy is gradually learning that you are fragile and that he must treat your skin with more respect than that of his furry friends. I will show you an exercise to achieve an end to all mouthing in Chapter 19, 'Being polite', but for the time being, concentrate on reducing the pressure of your puppy's bites. Let your puppy know that you are becoming more and more sensitive, so that by the time he is approaching four months old, he simply mouths gently at your fingers without causing you any pain.

Biting should be redirected onto appropriate toys.

Overexcitement

Puppies are more likely to bite hard and play too roughly when they are overexcited. Managing a puppy's arousal or excitement levels is very important, and overexcitement generally is a huge problem for some new puppy owners, especially where physical play is involved. Sometimes an overexcited puppy may behave in a way that gives his owners genuine cause for concern.

Symptoms of overexcitement that people tend to worry about include the puppy racing around at huge speed, bottom tucked beneath him, wild eyed and seemingly oblivious to everyone around him. The puppy may become so overwrought that he appears hysterical or demented, crashing into walls and sending tables and chairs flying. This is

Sometimes he just needs a moment to calm down.

not a sign that he is mentally ill, but it *is* a sign that he needs to be helped to calm down. If your tiny puppy has wound himself into a frenzy, scoop him up into your arms and hold him firmly. Take him away from any noise and excitement and talk to him very quietly and calmly. It may help simply to place him in his crate to calm down. Drawing the curtains, or throwing an old towel over the crate and leaving the room will help give the puppy a chance to recover.

IMPORTANT NOTE: Occasionally, a puppy will begin to growl and guard his food while he is eating. Don't worry, this is not abnormal and is easy to resolve. Don't punish him, just head straight for Part Three, Chapter 24, 'Guarding food', to find out what to do.

Lines of communication

Biting is often more of a problem than new puppy owners anticipate, but if managed carefully it should be a short-lived one. It is important to avoid getting a puppy overexcited not only because this is often when biting gets out of hand, but also because a puppy needs to be relatively calm in order to respond to, and communicate with, those around him. This may mean putting limits on physical playtime and concentrating on other ways of interacting with the puppy.

As our puppies mature and we focus increasingly on training and obedience, maintaining a great channel of communication between us becomes even more important. Some of the ways in which we expect our dogs to behave do not come naturally to puppies, and need a little explanation. In addition to keeping your puppy fairly calm, you will need some tools and strategies to help him understand what the humans around him actually expect him to do.

In the next chapter, we look at bridging the language barrier that exists between man and dog, to enable you to establish a great relationship with your puppy, built on mutual understanding and affection.

SUMMARY
- It is normal for puppies to growl ferociously and bite hard when playing.
- Stop playing with your puppy when he bites.
- Put him in his den with a chew toy.
- If he's overexcited, give him time to calm down.

18

Communication and bonding

As we begin to focus increasingly on training your rapidly developing puppy, we need to be sure that you and he are on the same wavelength. Dogs communicate primarily through body language, so when we train a puppy using verbal language or other audible signals, we are teaching him to communicate in a way that is essentially alien to him. Fortunately, dogs love learning, and there are some useful strategies and tools available to you to help you cross the language barrier that exists between you and your dog.

We talked in Part One about the importance of controlling the consequences of your puppy's actions in order to create permanent and persistent changes in his behaviour. In this chapter we will look at the practical steps we can take to control these consequences, including the application of rewards, and the management of your dog's environment. We will look at the way in which this control builds up a bond between you and your dog, and at other ways of deepening the bond between you. In the next chapter, we will be looking at modifying some common and inappropriate puppy behaviours using these tools and strategies. In the final chapter of Part Two, we will talk about the more structured and formal training we call 'obedience'.

The timing of rewards

Rewards are a powerful communication tool. They tell a puppy in no uncertain terms that this behaviour, this thing he just did, is valuable to you. Rewards let the puppy know he did the right thing. They provide that all-important positive consequence to desirable behaviours, and reinforce those behaviours so that your puppy will repeat them in the future. But, no matter how generously or effectively you reward a puppy, if your timing is poor, the puppy will struggle to understand what you are trying to teach him. It can be very difficult

Not all puppies appreciate a bath.

to deliver a reward to a dog in an accurate and timely manner, especially when he is not right next to you. Fortunately, we have an excellent tool that enables us to overcome this problem. It is called an event marker.

Using event markers

An event marker is a brief signal that you give your puppy, which 'marks' the action or behaviour that you want him to repeat. Many puppy owners struggle with training simply because their puppy is not clear on what he is required to do. An event marker neatly resolves any confusion on this score. If you are trying to teach a high five, you mark the moment that the puppy lifts up his paw. If you are trying to teach a puppy to be quiet, you mark the moment he stops making a noise and falls silent. Rewarding a puppy is fairly pointless unless he knows what the reward is for, and in many cases that information is *only* available to him if you use an event marker.

The most commonly used event marker in dog training is the clicker. Cheap and portable, it makes a consistent and distinctive sound that dogs find easy to identify and work with. I recommend you buy one before you go much further. You can use a word, such as 'good' or 'yes' if you prefer, and when you need both hands, a verbal event marker is useful. But for shaping new behaviours, such as walking at heel, and for teaching tricks, a clicker is the best tool.

🐾 The right rewards

An event marker is a very effective tool provided that you always, or nearly always, follow it with an effective reward. This is because the event marker itself becomes conditioned to give the dog a feeling of pleasure by frequent association with the reward itself.

Remember that the dog determines the right rewards; they must be valuable to him. Toys and games, such as retrieving, are wonderful rewards for more advanced training. Attention and interaction are often the best rewards for training alternatives to attention-seeking behaviours, such as whining, but for early training of new skills, there is little to beat food. It is portable and rapidly delivered. Your dog can swallow a cube of cheese in less than a second, whereas it might take him a minute or two to fetch his ball. Food is therefore the reward of choice for many types of puppy training, and you need to make sure that it is easily available.

Treat bag and box

With some types of training all you need is a pot of treats placed on the table. You might also find a couple of tiny Tupperware-type boxes handy. These can be used to store little cubes of cheese, or tiny pieces of left-over Sunday roast, in the fridge. But for outdoor training, or circumstances in which you are going to be moving about, you will need the treats attached to your person! I use bum-bags with a wipeable lining for my dog-training treats but you can use a pocket or some other kind of treat bag if you prefer. It is helpful if the bags are machine washable.

Reducing rewards

When you are teaching a puppy to respond to a signal, and once the puppy has grasped his new skill and is responding reliably to your cue, it is important to reward him in a random and unpredictable manner, gradually reducing the frequency and value of the rewards over a number of training sessions. Random and unpredictable rewards are more powerful reinforcers of behaviour in the long term. Remember to reward all desirable behaviours occasionally, or they will eventually become extinct.

Rewards and event markers help us to reinforce behaviour that we want to encourage. But we also need ways in which to trigger behaviours, so that we can ask a puppy to carry out specific requests at specific times.

Using signals

Verbal commands, hand signals and whistles are commonly used in dog training. Your signal is the dog's cue to respond, and different types of signals have their own advantages. The sound of a whistle has the advantage of being very consistent and carrying well outdoors, even in windy weather. Verbal commands, on the other hand, cannot be accidentally left at home and, of course, are more appropriate for many indoor-training activities.

Dogs can learn to respond in the same way to many different signals, so you don't need to worry that if you teach your puppy to recall to a whistle, you won't be able to teach him to recall to the word 'come'. It is probably best, however, to train your dog to respond to one signal reliably before adding a second. With all signals, the most important thing to remember is to give the signal once only. Repeating your signals teaches a puppy to ignore the first, second and even third.

Before you begin training, it is important to be clear on the distinction between the event marker (which can be a click or a word) and the cue (which is usually a whistle or a word). These are both signals, both ways of communicating with a puppy, but they serve very different purposes. The event marker identifies what the puppy did to earn his reward. The whistle (or verbal signal) cues the dog to respond with a specific action.

In the pages that follow you will find a number of exercises to get you started with training your puppy. Once you have worked through these, you will have the skills you need to invent a few of your own. However, it is important to remember that there is more to communication than just words, whistles and rewards. You will find training your dog a great deal easier if you have a good relationship with him, and have earned his attention and willingness to be with you. It is important that your puppy takes pleasure in your company. This is what we mean by building a bond with your dog.

The bond between you

The bond between an owner and his dog is forged through shared activities, resources and companionship. Managing a puppy's time outdoors is a crucial part of building that bond. A puppy left to his own devices on a walk soon learns that you are boring and that he needs to find his own amusement. A puppy that is constantly interacting with his owner outdoors, through ball games and training exercises, becomes deeply fascinated by his human friend.

You can build a strong connection with your puppy at home, too. Make sure you always have a few pieces of kibble in your pocket, and reward your puppy often for seeking out your company. Whenever he approaches you of his own accord, say his name and give him a little piece of kibble or cheese. He will soon be looking for you every time he hears you say his name.

To build a really strong bond with your puppy, it is important that you are the centre of his world, and that he spends more meaningful time with you than he does with other companions. If you have an older dog at home who enjoys playing with the puppy, your little one will get plenty of exercise this way, but it is important to place some restrictions on the amount of time the two dogs spend playing together. Puppies that are allowed close contact with other dogs for long periods of time sometimes become bonded to the older dog, to the detriment of the bond with the owner.

Physical contact is important to dogs and your dog should get the majority of his physical contact from you, rather than from other dogs. Regular grooming sessions can be an important part of this process.

Grooming and handling

If your puppy is a long-haired breed, you will need to pay attention to his coat in order to avoid tangles and matting, especially around the ears and the tops of the back legs. But even if your dog's coat needs little attention, grooming can play an important role in the relationship between you, as most dogs find regular brushing or massaging extremely soothing and calming.

Having fun together helps you bond with your dog.

People sometimes ask, 'How often should I bath my puppy?' Puppies don't need bathing at all unless they get particularly grubby, and frequent shampooing probably does not benefit a dog's coat as it may strip out the natural oils. It is still worthwhile getting puppies accustomed to the occasional bath, though, because you never know when he might need one in the future. Dogs that are not accustomed to being soaked and shampooed as puppies may find it quite an unnerving experience at a later date.

Grooming is a bonding activity but it is also an important learning process for all puppies. Part of being a well-mannered dog is a willingness to be handled and touched all over. Dogs that are not used to such handling as puppies may never appreciate it in quite the same way when they are older. Don't forget to examine your puppy's feet and ears regularly as a part of your grooming routine, so that he is comfortable with this kind of personal contact.

Grooming helps to deepen the bond between you and your puppy.

Long-eared puppies must be happy to have their ears groomed and examined.

The polite puppy

Choosing the right rewards and using an event marker are important aids in educating puppies. Reinforcing good behaviour, together with an effective strategy for managing your puppy outdoors and building a bond between you, lie at the heart of a rich and rewarding relationship between you and your dog, and pave the way for success in training.

We tend to think of dog training in terms of teaching dogs to respond to specific commands, such as sit, come, heel and down. These are important skills for every dog to learn, and we will take a look at getting started with obedience training in the final chapter of this section. But much of early puppy training is actually about teaching puppies to respond appropriately to specific situations, rather than to commands. Most of us want our puppies to be polite. Training your puppy to respond appropriately to different situations as they arise gives him good manners. You will be raising a polite puppy, and that is the topic of our next chapter.

 SUMMARY
- Timing is all important.
- Use event markers to tell your puppy he's doing the right thing.
- Reinforce wanted behaviours with valuable rewards.
- Nurture the bond between you and your puppy by grooming and handling him regularly.

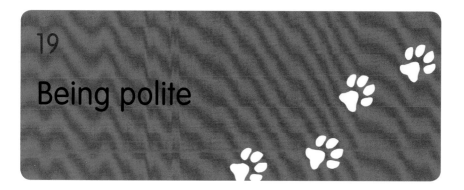

19
Being polite

We are a pretty tolerant society when it comes to dogs. On balance, most people like them, though of course we all have differing views about what constitutes a well-behaved dog. Some people are happy to have a large dog put his paws on their shoulders; others are not so keen. Some don't mind eating their dinner next to a dog that is staring at their plate with a long string of saliva dangling from the side of his mouth. Others feel differently.

Even though we each have our own ideas about what a well-behaved dog should do or be, there is probably quite a lot of common ground between us. In this chapter we are going to look at some behaviours that many people find objectionable. We'll cover putting an end to mouthing, jumping up and snatching, and also teach your dog how to be very polite and say 'please' when he wants something.

An end to biting and mouthing

Many small puppies grab at any outstretched hand with their mouths. This technique to stop him from doing that can also be used with older puppies that nip at outstretched hands, and it is a good exercise to do before moving on to the learning not to snatch exercise on the next page.

What you are going to do is simply to reward the puppy for keeping his mouth away from your hands. An ideal alternative behaviour to look for is the puppy gazing into your face while ignoring your hands. You may find it easier in this case to use a verbal event marker to pinpoint the correct behaviour, since both your hands will be busy. The event marker in the example on the next page is the word 'good'.

The starting position is for you to have both hands at your waistline with the puppy in front of you. You can drop a few treats first to get him interested.

1. Hold some treats in one hand and move the other hand towards the puppy – do not touch him.
2. If he does *not* move his mouth towards your hand, say 'good', drop him a treat with the other hand, and return both hands to your waist.
3. Repeat several times.
4. Switch hands and repeat.

The chances are that he *will* move his head towards your hand. If so, you need to simplify the exercise.

Simplifying the exercise

Do this by making much smaller movements of your hand to begin with. Have both hands loosely clasped at your waist and just waggle *one hand* slightly. Say 'good' and treat the puppy for looking at your face rather than your hand.

Now progress to moving your hand just a little way towards the puppy. Keep increasing your hand movements and rewarding him for ignoring them. This may take a few days of twice daily sessions.

Progressing the exercise

When your puppy is able to resist reaching his mouth towards your fully extended hand, you can repeat the exercise but this time begin lightly touching his body. With practice, you will soon be able to touch his sides, back, tail, and even face, without him turning to grasp at your fingers.

Practise this a lot in different places until you can touch and handle your puppy freely anywhere, without him grabbing or nipping at your fingers. If your puppy is kibble fed and still very bitey at twelve weeks or so, you can use his entire daily food ration to get this sorted out.

🐾 Learning not to snatch

Many puppies that have learned not to bite in play still snatch food when it is offered from an outstretched hand, often grabbing fingers in the process. This can be very painful indeed, as the puppy is not inhibiting his bite when he is eating. It is also very rude. This exercise will put a stop to painful snatching and teach your puppy to take food politely and gently from your hand. Have a pot of treats ready nearby, and a single treat in one hand. Let your puppy see that you have a treat in your hand and close your fist around it. Be ready to mark the right behaviour using a clicker or the word 'good'.

1. Stretch out your arm so that your fist is in front of the puppy's nose. Don't open your fist yet. Most puppies will poke and paw at your fist, then back off.
2. Mark the moment when the puppy backs off.
3. Feed the puppy a different treat from the other hand.
4. Repeat until the puppy quickly backs off each time you present your fist, and waits for you to respond.

He'll sniff at your hand.

Puppies catch on very quickly to this, but you need to avoid some common mistakes. You can easily get into a little pattern of the puppy touching, then backing away, then touching again if he thinks that is what is triggering the reward. What we actually want is for him to make no attempt to touch your fist at all as you move your hand towards him. One way to achieve this is to mark and reward him several times in succession as he backs off and before he touches you again. Another is to mark and reward him as you extend your fist towards him and *before* he attempts to touch it. It is similar to the previous exercise. Try to think of it as rewarding him for keeping his head still and not moving it towards you.

He may paw at your hand to try and reach the treat.

The next step is to teach him not to touch your fist as you uncurl your hand. You will need to be quick and curl your fingers up again if he makes a move. Always reward him from the *other hand* using a treat from your pot. Don't let him have the treat in your fist yet. When you can hold your outstretched palm in front of him without him touching the treat, you can give this self-control a name. I use 'leave it'. When he is familiar with the words 'leave it' you can teach him the opposite, 'take it'. This is simple. Just press the palm of your hand with the treat in right up against his lips and say 'take it' in a happy and upbeat way.

As soon as he backs away, mark and reward!

IMPORTANT NOTE: For several weeks, make sure you do at least ten repetitions of a 'leave it' for every 'take it' or your new behaviour will break down.

🐾 No more jumping up

Almost all puppies quickly learn to jump up at people. What your puppy wants is to get near to your face, and as he is small and you are tall, jumping up is rewarding for him. The fact that everyone who comes to see him will make a fuss of him for jumping up simply reinforces for him that jumping up is a great idea. If you have a very small breed of dog, you might not mind this, although even small muddy paws can make a mess of smart clothes. But for most dog owners, stopping their dog from jumping up is quite a priority.

Nowadays we teach dogs not to jump up in two ways. Firstly, we remove all reinforcement for jumping up so that the behaviour can become extinct, and secondly, we teach him an alternative and more acceptable behaviour for greeting people.

Four on the floor

It goes without saying that your puppy cannot jump up and keep four paws on the floor at the same time. Keeping all four feet on the ground is your alternative behaviour. This is what you want the puppy to do when people touch and pet him. If all jumping up is ignored and a puppy is rewarded for keeping his feet on the ground, the jumping up *will* stop. But this takes time. The sooner you start teaching 'four on the floor' the better. One of the best rewards you can use for a small puppy is your attention. So if he puts his feet on you when you stroke him, stop stroking. When he puts his feet back down on the floor again, stroke him once more. Just as in the previous exercises, it is useful to mark the behaviour you like so that your puppy knows what you are rewarding him for. You can do this with your clicker or with your marker word, 'good'. If your puppy jumps up a lot, you will need to set up training sessions to help him learn not to do this. If you are using food rewards, place the treats on the *floor* so that he is looking down for his rewards, and is not tempted to jump up towards your hands.

You can do this as visitors arrive if you prime them to ignore the puppy when he jumps up. Wait by the door with lots of treats and be ready to feed the puppy multiple times as the visitors come in. Feeding too slowly is where many people fall down. If you leave too long between treats, he will be distracted by your visitors. Repeatedly mark him for having four feet on the ground and reward after every single mark. Place each treat on the floor, and repeat often.

It is a good idea to teach alternatives to jumping up for attention.

If you know that your visitors will undermine your efforts by rewarding any jumping up, make sure your puppy is in his crate before you let them in. Consistency is very important.

Learning to say please

Well-behaved dogs are likeable dogs and we all want our dogs to be liked. We want to be proud of our four-legged friend. One of the best ways to achieve this is to make sure that your dog is demonstrably well mannered. Saying please is

A well-behaved puppy sits to say please.

a clear demonstration of good manners. We teach our children at an early age to say 'please' when they want something, but dogs are hampered by a lack of language. What your puppy needs is way of saying 'please' that is instantly recognisable and socially acceptable. This is actually a very simple thing to teach. We just need to replace the word 'please' with a sit.

It is widely recognised by human beings that a dog sitting directly in front of you and looking into your eyes is asking for something. Many dogs figure this out for themselves, but you can give your puppy a head start by teaching him to do it from the beginning. A sit command is one of the most useful ways of communicating with a dog, and we'll look at teaching it in the next chapter. But the sit to say please needs no command or signal.

Teaching a puppy to sit to say please gives you all kinds of opportunities to be creative with rewards. Many opportunities to reward our puppies occur every single day, most of which we never use. Think about all the things your puppy likes and enjoys. Eating his dinner is an obvious one, but what about having his ears stroked, seeing his lead taken down from the hook in the hall, the jangle of your car keys predicting a ride to the woods, or the sight of his ball in your hands? You can make all these rewards dependent on a sit.

Whenever you see your puppy doing something you don't like, you need to decide what you would like him to do instead, and in many cases a sit is the ideal substitute. Encourage your puppy to sit by the door rather than scratch at it, for example, and to sit next to things that he wants.

This is not about training obedience to the sit command. Don't *ask* or *tell* your puppy to sit yet. Just wait until he does so. If you *tell* him to sit, he is not working out for himself how to say 'please'. And if he disobeys you, the word 'sit' will have lost all its potential power.

Onwards to obedience

The first month or so with a new puppy in the house is a bit of a whirlwind. But by the time our youngsters are three months old, life has usually assumed some semblance of normality. As you pass the three-month mark and head towards your puppy's four-month birthday, you will be leaving behind some of the problems of early puppyhood, and will have settled into a routine with your new friend.

There will, of course, be some new and different challenges ahead to keep you on your toes, and many puppy owners by this point, watching their tiny puppy grow at an alarming rate, will have begun to think seriously about the question of obedience training. This is the focus of the final chapter in Part Two of this book.

SUMMARY

- Replace objectionable behaviours with alternative, more desirable ones.
- Use markers and rewards to guide your puppy and practise frequently.
- Use his entire daily food ration in rewards if necessary.
- Encourage your puppy to sit when he wants something.

20
Towards obedience

You will probably have seen dogs appearing on talent shows on TV. These displays demonstrate just what a variety of commands and different skills a dog is capable of learning, even memorising quite complex chains of behaviour. Most of us don't require our dogs to turn somersaults, dance or jump through hoops, but it is inspiring to see the potential for learning that is there. Potential is something your puppy has plenty of, and you will naturally want to make the most of it. At times it can seem an overwhelming task and you may be unsure where to begin.

A lot of unnecessary mystique surrounds dog training. The skills and timing of experienced trainers can make those watching feel incompetent. I want *you* to know that almost anyone can train a dog to a high standard if provided with the right information. You do not need any kind of special attributes or skills to make a good job of training your puppy. You can have the well-trained dog of your dreams in exchange for nothing more than a little of your time. Obedience training is a big subject and this chapter is not intended to be a comprehensive dog-training manual. What I aim to do is give you the tools that you need to set you off on the right path to teaching your puppy how to respond reliably to your commands. We'll start by taking a look at the skills you need to teach your dog for safety's sake and to ensure he will be welcome everywhere he goes.

Safety first

Your puppy is not capable of making the judgements necessary to protect himself in our urban world, and he never will be. Unlike your children, your puppy will never become independent or leave home. For him to be safe, unleashed, outdoors for the rest of his life, he needs to learn to come running whenever you call him. And for both of you to be safe when he is on a lead, he needs to learn to walk next to you, without choking himself on his collar or dragging you under a passing bus.

So, the two key safety skills you will need to teach your dog in order to keep him (and those around him) safe are recall, and walking on a loose lead, or what trainers refer to as walking to heel. Before we look at some training exercises, I want to talk about the stages in training that you will need to work through.

The five stages in training

What we all want to achieve when we teach a dog to react to our commands is a trained response. The trained response does not involve decisions or choices. It is an action that the dog makes automatically upon hearing or seeing a cue or signal that his handler gives to him. We use rewards to establish the response, and once fully trained, the dog makes this response without hesitation and without knowing whether or not he will receive a reward.

There are five key stages in creating a trained response, and these are:

1. Establish the behaviour.
2. Pair the desired behaviour with a signal.
3. Teach the dog to respond to the signal.
4. Proof the new response against distractions.
5. Maintain the trained response for all time.

These are the stages that *modern* dog training uses. Traditional-style training starts at stage three, but we now know that the first two stages make the process a whole lot easier on both you and your dog. Let's take a closer look at each stage in turn.

Stage one: establish the behaviour

You are already familiar with this stage in training. We have looked at working through stage one with two skills – recall and sit (pages 128 and 156). You already know how to get your puppy running towards you, and how to get your puppy to sit by rewarding him repeatedly for doing so.

There are no commands or cues in stage one – just actions and rewards. If you have been practising the puppy recall and the sit to say please for a while, you may now have a puppy that finds it rewarding to rush towards you, and sits whenever he wants to be rewarded. It is important to spend a little time on this stage in training if you haven't yet done so.

Getting your puppy to walk next to you in exchange for rewards is the first stage in heelwork training, and we'll take a look at that now.

Establishing heel

Work with your puppy in a confined area, such as a large room indoors, or a small enclosed garden. Just as in all basic training, you need to be *free from distractions* and to have some edible rewards, and you need an event marker, such as a clicker.

All you need to do is wander about in your enclosed area while imagining a circle on the ground that is attached to your left leg. The circle should be a few feet across, and each time the puppy wanders into it, you press your clicker or give your verbal event marker 'good'.

1. Wander about in your enclosed area.
2. Click each time the puppy enters your circle. Keep moving!
3. Throw the treat outside the circle and repeat.

What could be simpler? The puppy will soon be rushing back into your circle, expecting you to throw another treat. Over a session or two, start to shrink the size of your imaginary circle, always ensuring that the edge of it remains firmly attached to your left foot.

Puppies can be taught from an early age to walk next to your left leg.

Within a very short space of time your puppy will be rushing into the heel position after collecting his treat. Your next task is to build some duration on to this behaviour by walking two steps with him at heel before you click and treat, then three steps. Build up slowly to five steps. Now you are ready to move on to stage two.

Stage two: pair the behaviour with a signal

Stage two in dog training is building an association in your dog's mind between the action you want him to carry out and the word or signal you will be using to trigger or cue this desirable behaviour. We introduce our cue word *while the action is occurring and not before*. I gave you an example of this in Chapter 15, 'Beginning the puppy recall'. Exercise two (pages 130–31) showed you how to pair the recall signal with the action of running towards you. We can add this stage now to our sit training. Next time your puppy is waiting by the door to go out into the garden, say 'sit' just as he sits to say please. Try to time it so you say the word exactly as his bottom moves towards the floor. If he changes his mind and does not sit, do not open the door! And do not repeat the word. Just wait for him to sit properly and let him out immediately. Do the same with any other rewards that your puppy has learned to sit for. Don't repeat the word 'sit' a second time, and do give the puppy his reward immediately. You can do the same with your heel cue. Each time the puppy falls into place by your left leg, just quietly say 'heel'.

When you have paired your signal with your dog's actions for several training sessions, spaced out over several days, you are ready to give stage three a go!

Stage three: teach the dog to respond

At this stage, we introduce the signal as a *cue* for the behaviour to begin. So instead of just pairing your whistle or command with the behaviour, we are going to use it as a signal to trigger the action we require. You'll be saying the word 'come' or 'sit' or 'heel', and your puppy will run towards you, or sit, or fall into place next to your leg.

He'll be doing these things under very controlled conditions, where there are no distractions, but these are the building blocks of your puppy's future training, and it pays to make sure he is repeatedly successful. Sometimes we need to break this stage down into sections, and start by giving the puppy lots of additional encouragement after our cue, to ensure that he doesn't fail. Let's look at how we can apply stage three to the recall. We are going to divide this into two exercises, recall and run, and recall and stand.

Recall and run

The sight of you running away from the puppy is still a part of the process at this point. As soon as he hears your whistle, we want the puppy to look up and see you racing away from him. We don't want him to have a second to consider his response, we just want him to start chasing you immediately.

1. Put the puppy on the ground.
2. Make some distance between you.
3. Give your recall signal *before* he starts to move towards you, and run away from the puppy.
4. Glance over your shoulder and make sure he is following you.
5. If he has not noticed you running away, clap your hands, squeak and whoop – whatever it takes to attract his attention and get him to chase you.
6. Reward generously when he arrives.

It really is important for your puppy to run after you at this point. So do whatever is necessary, no matter how silly you may feel. If the puppy shows any lack of enthusiasm for this game, arm yourself with some very tasty food rewards and use them generously until you get a rapid and enthusiastic response to every single recall.

Once you are confident that the puppy is chasing after you reliably every time you call, you should start rewarding him intermittently for a few days before moving on to the next exercise. Spend a week or two working on this. Make sure you practise every day, several times a day.

Recall and stand

The next stage is to teach your puppy to come to you without the extra incentive of watching you disappear from view. Before you start teaching this stage, make sure that your puppy is very competent at the recall and run – and make sure you have some good rewards with you before you start the game.

1. Put the puppy on the ground.
2. Make some distance between you.
3. Give your recall signal and stand still.
4. Crouch down as the puppy reaches you and reward generously when he arrives.

If your puppy does not run towards you, without hesitation, run away, clap your hands, squeak and whoop – as before, do whatever it takes to attract his

Now it's time to keep still whilst you call your puppy.

attention and get him chasing you. Then work some more on recall and run *before* trying this exercise again. It is vital at this stage to work well away from distractions. Do not be tempted to test the puppy when he is playing, or wanting to play, with other people or dogs. Make sure you are completely undisturbed while you establish this new response.

You can apply these same principles to your trained sit.

Sit when I say 'sit'

1. Pick a time when you will not be disturbed.
2. Put some treats in a pot in an easily accessible place.
3. If he spots you doing this, wait for the puppy to forget about them.
4. When the puppy is standing around doing nothing in particular, wait for him to look at you, and say 'sit'.
5. Now wait.
6. If he sits, reward generously.

If he does not sit, do not say another word, just fetch a treat from the pot and lure him into the sit position by holding it above his nose and moving it backwards. Then mark his position with the clicker or your special word, and reward him with the treat.

If you experience failure at this stage, don't keep trying today. Go back to stage two for a while, then try again. He will understand sooner than you think. Use the same technique with heel. Walk away from your puppy and say 'heel' as you do so. If he falls into place beside you, reward immediately and profusely. Don't wait to get your five steps in; you can build these up again once you have a nice response to your 'heel' cue. When you get to this point, it is a simple matter to attach a lead to your puppy's collar, or pop a slip lead over his head. Puppies that are taught using this method may never experience what it means to pull on a lead in their lives.

Once your puppy responds reliably and quickly to your new commands where there are no distractions, it is time to move on to stage four.

Stage four: proof the response

Proofing means teaching your puppy to respond to a signal *no matter what else is happening* around him. This is by far the longest part of the training process and the part of puppy training that most people miss out or skim over. It comes as a shock to many new puppy owners to find that their puppy pays absolutely no attention to any commands whatsoever when they take him to a public place, or when a friend comes to visit. This is not naughtiness; it is normal.

A dog needs to be taught that a new command applies in a whole range of different situations. This process will take you much of the first year of your dog's life. You will be gradually adding factors of difficulty and increasingly challenging distractions to your dog's environment while expecting him to respond to your cues.

Proofing needs to be age appropriate. As your puppy approaches four months old, he is beginning to develop the ability to concentrate a little longer on his

his lessons. You can start to add tiny periods of proofing to his training sessions. Start small, keep lessons short and build up slowly. For example, you can begin to increase the duration of his sit, and to recall him from farther away. We often refer to the long-duration sit as a 'stay' but you do not need the added complication of a stay command. Just gradually increase the length of time you wait before marking and rewarding the sit, by a second or two each time. You can ask the puppy to walk to heel for longer distances, but don't make this too difficult, and break it up with sits – five paces, then a sit, then five more paces and another sit. A ten-second sit is great, but asking a four-month-old puppy to sit for two minutes is setting him up to fail.

Asking a puppy to sit still while you move away from him adds another level of difficulty, so don't introduce this until you have built some duration into the sit with the puppy at your side. And always return to the puppy at the end of the stay or he will begin pre-empting your recall.

To proof your training effectively, you will need to:

- Build up duration and other levels of difficulty gradually.
- Introduce distractions one at a time and at low levels to begin with.
- Prevent the puppy from helping himself to rewards for bad behaviour.
- Use more powerful rewards for new or more difficult tasks.

Build up the duration of the 'stay' gradually.

Most young puppies will not *at first* be able to sit and stay while another dog plays or runs around nearby. So introduce the distraction of other dogs in a low-key and achievable way. Fade rewards down to an occasional treat before attempting to move on to a more difficult exercise.

Proofing needs to be thorough if training is not to break down later. You can find lots of exercises for proofing your new recall command in my book *Total Recall* (details in the resources section), but the most important thing to remember whether you are teaching recall, or any other skill, is that distractions of any kind must be introduced gradually.

Stage five: maintain the response

Once your puppy's trained response has been taught and proofed, it is a relatively simple task to maintain it. Responses may get sloppy over time simply because we are human and we get sloppy, too. Remembering to reward your dog from time to time and to interact with him outdoors are the keys to maintaining most behaviours and keeping your relationship fresh. If you make yourself an interesting walking partner, it will go a long way towards keeping your puppy focused on you and happy to be near you.

The good citizen

The objective of training your puppy is to keep him safe and to help him be a good canine citizen. If you enjoy training your puppy, you might like to enrol in the Kennel Club's good citizen dog-training scheme. The scheme offers awards at three levels, bronze, silver and gold. You can find out all about it on the Kennel Club's website and there are training classes in many locations across the country. If you own a gundog breed puppy, you can join the Graded Training Scheme for pet and working gundogs, provided by the Gundog Club. Contact details for the Kennel Club and the Gundog Club are at the back of this book.

Being a good citizen, of course, involves more than a few awards. The aim is to own a dog that is a pleasure to be around, and under control at all times. When you call your dog, you want him to race towards you without a moment's hesitation, even when there are other dogs to play with, ice creams to steal and seagulls to annoy. You want your dog to be welcome at your friend's birthday party, or in the local pub, to be a dog that people want to spend time with. Training your puppy requires some time and effort, but the rewards are great – for him as well as for you.

Take your time and proof your recall thoroughly.

🐾 Your journey

We have come to the end of Part Two of this book and I hope that you have found it helpful. There are some chapters in Part Three for those of you who have a problem with a particular aspect of your puppy's behaviour, and you will find a list of further resources to help you with your puppy in the back of this book.

Raising a puppy is quite a journey, one that many have made before you. Dogs have been in partnership with mankind since before the dawn of agriculture. We've climbed mountains and fought wars together, and been hurtled into the technological age, still together. It's been quite a ride! The effects and implications of such a long and unique partnership between two very different species are still being unravelled and revealed. We may know a lot more about dogs than our grandfathers did, but there is so much yet to discover.

Every puppy provides a wonderful opportunity to start the journey afresh, to build an unshakeable friendship, and to learn about these extraordinary animals that share our homes and daily lives. Enjoy every second you spend with your happy puppy, and revel in the relationship you build together. He will provide you with a few challenges along the way but will reward your efforts a thousand-fold with his unconditional loyalty and devotion.

 SUMMARY

- Focus on achieving a trained response to important signals.
- Begin training in a quiet place with no distractions.
- For your puppy, training is a game.
- Make sure your puppy is proficient at each of the five stages of training before moving on to the next one.
- Introduce distractions gradually.

Part Three

Problem solving

21

The noisy puppy

D ealing with a noisy puppy can be very stressful. Not only has your peace and quiet been shattered, you may be worried about what the future holds. Most new puppy owners are aware that noisy puppies have the potential to grow into noisy dogs, and while noisy puppies can be quite cute, the adult version is rarely so appealing. If your puppy screams the house down each time you step out of the room, your relationship with close neighbours will undoubtedly be strained. There is only so much goodwill you can win with wine, chocolates and apologies.

Very tiny puppies will cry when they are left alone in their new homes because they are afraid. This is natural and normal, and generally does not last more than a few days. But within a very short space of time, a new and different sort of crying may begin. If your puppy has been with you for much more than a week and is making a lot of noise, the chances are he has learned to cry or bark in order to gain attention, company or some other resource that he knows you can provide, such as dinner, or a romp in the garden.

He might be cute, but he can make a lot of noise!

🐾 Being alone

All puppies need to learn to spend short periods of time on their own. If your puppy howls his head off when you go to the bathroom, or pop out to the shops, you are right to be worried. If he whines constantly when you are on the phone, yaps continuously while you prepare his meals, and yells every time he is popped into his crate, then you have the beginnings of a problem. Now is the time to take action. Don't wait to see if your puppy will grow out of it. He probably won't.

We have talked quite a bit about accidental learning, and you will almost certainly realise that you have contributed to the noises that your puppy is making by accidentally reinforcing them. Fortunately, you can train the puppy to be quiet in the same way that you trained him to be noisy, by reinforcing quiet behaviour using powerful rewards. The technique I use teaches puppies to be quiet in simple stages. I call it 'click for quiet' and you really do need an accurate event marker, such as a clicker, for this task. (See Chapter 18, 'Communication and bonding', for more information on event markers.) This is because, to begin with, you are going to have to mark an extremely brief moment in time. Let's see how it works with a puppy that howls when he is shut in his crate.

Click for quiet

Teaching a screaming puppy that being quiet is a good thing might seem like an impossible task. How can we reward him for being quiet often enough to get a learning process under way, when all he does is yell? Fortunately, even the most determined puppy pauses for breath from time to time, and it is these small breaks in howling, these tiny moments of quiet, that we are going to capture with an event marker, and reward.

If you try to reward this break or pause in the howling without an event marker, there is a real risk that the puppy will start crying again just at the moment he gets his reward, which will, of course, reinforce the howling and make it worse. A clicker is the ideal event marker for this project, because it is so precise. The objective here is to wait for that pause in the howling, mark it with your click, then follow it rapidly with a reward. The reward can be anything that the puppy really desires. In some cases this will be as simple as letting him see that you have not abandoned him. In others cases it may mean letting the puppy out of the crate, or giving him a treat while he is still inside it. In this example we will use both the treat, and your presence.

Don't start this training late at night. Choose an early morning when you have the whole day ahead of you, so that you can make good progress by the evening.

The technique

Have your clicker ready, and some treats.

1. Place the puppy in his crate, and leave the room, closing the door behind you.
2. If the puppy does not start howling within three seconds, press the clicker and return to him. *Still return to him even if he has started crying again because the click identified for the puppy that it was his silence that earned him the reward of your return.*
3. Tell him what a clever dog he is, then leave the room again and close the door.
4. If the puppy starts howling after you leave him, and he probably will, listen to the pattern of howls and wait for a break.
5. Press that clicker in a moment of silence, and go straight in to him.
6. Give him a treat and tell him how great he is.
7. Then leave the room again, closing the door behind you.

Repeat ten to twenty times. Click and return to the puppy if he stays quiet for three seconds after you leave him. If he cries after you leave him, click and return to him when you hear a break in the howling. When you have completed at least ten repetitions, the next time you return to reward him, take him out of his crate, give him some time and attention, and an opportunity to go to the toilet.

Wait for your puppy to be quiet, then reward him.

Repeat the whole process half an hour or an hour later. Try to get five or more sessions in during the day. The more times you do this, the sooner the puppy will catch on.

Making progress

The way you make progress with this system is very straightforward. You simply increase the length of time you expect the puppy to be quiet, before rewarding him. The secret of success is to build up duration very gradually. So instead of waiting for three seconds of quiet after leaving the room, wait for four seconds, then five. Don't rush it. And instead of rewarding a split-second pause in the howling, wait for a two-second gap.

If you are struggling at any point, don't be afraid to go back to shorter gaps for a while. Success breeds success, and most puppies learn very quickly with this technique. You should see significant improvement within a day or two.

It is fine to use this technique with very small puppies. In fact, once the puppy has settled in towards the end of the first week, the sooner you start the better.

🐾 Early waking

One very common problem with older puppies is that they begin waking up earlier and earlier in the morning. This problem is often caused by the owner rushing to let the puppy out of his crate the very second they reach the kitchen. Your presence, and eventually just the sound of you moving around upstairs or of the central heating coming on, predicts the reward of being let out and so the puppy becomes excited. One morning he whines or barks and is rewarded by your presence, which reinforces the whining. And so the spiral of escalating noise begins.

The long-term solution to early morning attention barking is to ignore the puppy when you arrive in the kitchen. Don't look at him, don't talk to him, no good mornings, not even a scolding. Your presence should predict absolutely nothing to his benefit. Only when he is completely silent, do you go over to the crate and let him out. I do this with all my puppies once their bladder can cope, usually at about four months of age. Within a week or so, instead of charging around the crate with excitement when you enter the kitchen, your puppy will open one eye and then go back to sleep. If he is very overexcited, you may need to use the click-for-quiet technique to get this routine established.

Is he lonely?

A lot of people worry that their dog might be lonely at night. Some even have their dog sleeping on their bed so that he does not get upset. Letting your dog sleep on your bed is not a problem if that is how you like to spend your night, but there is no need to be concerned about a dog that sleeps downstairs alone. Remember that your dog has far better hearing than you do and an amazing sense of smell. He knows exactly where you are and can probably hear you snoring from his crate. Of course, he would prefer to sleep on your warm body, but he doesn't need to if you prefer to sleep in peace.

Barking with excitement

Some puppies will bark when they get overexcited. This might be while you are preparing a meal for them, getting ready to go for a walk, or while they are playing. The answer is to remove any rewards for excitable behaviour. If your puppy starts barking as you get out his dinner bowl, put it away again. Prepare his food a bit later while he is out in the garden or playing with your children. Surprise him with it. Don't let a puppy watch you and wind himself up. The same applies to having his lead put on. Placing a lead on a dog that knows he is about to go for a walk is very rewarding. Make sure you are rewarding the behaviour that you want, i.e. sitting quietly. Barking during play should result in the end of the game. You need to take control of this kind of behaviour at an early stage or it can escalate horribly.

Quiet in the car

Small puppies often cry in the car when first expected to travel in a car crate. You can use the click-for-quiet technique to teach a puppy to remain silent. Obviously, you can't reward the puppy by taking him out of the crate while you are driving, but you can reward him with the sound of your voice. If you take a friend along to pop a treat through the bars of his car crate, so much the better. You will have to use a word, such as 'yes' or 'good', for your event marker.

When he starts to cry in the car, everyone including any passengers must remain silent. Don't even talk to each other. When he pauses for breath, say 'yes' and tell him how great and clever he is in a very chirpy way. If you have a passenger, ask him or her to give the puppy a treat. Then carry on talking to each other as normal until he starts to whine or cry again. Gradually build up the time you expect him to be quiet before chatting to him or offering him a treat.

Destination excitement

Many dogs learn to scream or pace frantically in a car in anticipation of arrival. These are typically dogs that are always driven to their exercise area. The puppy quickly learns that certain twists and turns in the road predict a walk, and he becomes extremely excited about it. The whining and scrabbling that we see with destination excitement arise because we inadvertently reinforce the behaviour by the simple act of letting the puppy out of the car while he is being silly. To prevent and cure this problem, take a flask of coffee and a newspaper, and when you park the car at your walking spot, switch of the engine and read for twenty minutes until the dog has calmed down completely.

A quiet life

It is probably worth emphasising that many dogs are not particularly noisy by nature. We tend to make dogs noisy by accident. We are a chatty and friendly species and love nothing more than a bit of verbal communication. When puppies talk back, we often encourage them. 'What a clever dog!' 'Do you want your dinner then?' Before you know it, your puppy is yapping with excitement every time he sees his dinner bowl come out. Try hard to ignore little puppy noises and to reward him for silence. It won't make him sad – dogs are quite happy to communicate with gestures and touch – and it may make your life a lot easier in the months to come.

SUMMARY
- Mark and reward your puppy's silence, however brief.
- Do it often.
- Wait for increasingly longer silences before offering a reward.

22

Destructive behaviour

I t can be difficult to convince people of the need for restricting a puppy's access to parts of their home until they have seen with their own eyes what the effects of his attempts to help with their interior design actually look like.

Leaving your puppy alone in a nice room with beautiful furniture and expensive soft furnishings is about as sensible as taking your eyes off a toddler in a room containing both an antique quilt and a pair of strong kitchen scissors (I did this once). Your puppy's jaws are many times more powerful than your scissors. He can unstuff a cushion faster than you can blink, and he will not be using the zip. His ability to disassemble your children's most rugged and favourite toys has to be seen to be believed. And if he doesn't electrocute himself, or swallow something and choke, before he reaches his first birthday, you will have escaped lightly. My main task in this chapter is to convince you that no matter how destructive you think your puppy is, he is, in fact, completely normal.

All puppies like to chew things.

Teething

During the first few months of his life, your puppy's baby teeth will be replaced with a blunter and less painful set of adult ones. To ease the passage of his new teeth into this world, he will want to spend a good deal of his time chewing anything he can fit into his mouth. He isn't fussy about how much these items are worth or to whom they belong. Anything in his reach is fair game. Your role is to persuade him to chew items purchased for this purpose. His role is not to care. The two of you are never going to agree on a suitable chew toy, so you will need to be conscientious about keeping things you don't want him to have right out of his way.

Trying to teach a puppy not to chew things you don't want him to have is impractical, simply because there are so many of them. Where would you begin? You may be tempted to punish the puppy, but this just teaches him to be sneaky about chewing, not that chewing is wrong. The only sensible solution is to teach him what he *can* have, move everything else out of his way, and deny him access to rooms where there is a high proportion of valuable stuff unless he is under the direct supervision of an adult. I say adult because teenagers think supervising a puppy means glancing at him every ten minutes and shouting 'Mu-um' when he eats a firelighter.

Kongs and chews

If you have not yet purchased some Kongs, don't waste another moment. Just order yourself three Kongs right now. Fill them with mushy puppy food and freeze them. Every time you need to redirect your puppy away from chewing your possessions, give him a frozen filled-Kong to chew. Kongs are one of the few chew toys that you can leave a puppy with unsupervised. They are incredibly tough and, provided you get one big enough for your puppy, he won't be able to break or swallow it. Other chew toys will help to ease your puppy's craving for something to chew, but these do need supervision.

Not all puppies are as gentle with soft toys as this young Viszla.

Don't let your puppy wander off with a rawhide chew stick. He will quickly break lumps off and swallow them, which will make him sick, or get bits stuck in his throat. When your puppy is a bit bigger, you can buy him a giant rawhide bone, which he can gnaw on in his basket while you eat your supper. You don't need to hold the end, but you will need to keep an eye on it for signs that he has softened it up enough to pull bits off. Take it away from him when you go out, and throw it away when it starts to come apart.

🐾 When you cannot supervise

At these times, pop your puppy into his crate for a few minutes. Some puppies can be left un-crated without wreaking havoc, but their owners are probably not reading this chapter. If you are struggling with a destructive puppy, intervals in the crate are a lifesaver. You simply cannot watch the puppy all the time.

Balls intended for children may not last long.

Many people who have problems with a puppy chewing up their homes have tried to de-crate their puppy at night and give him his freedom at far too young an age. This is especially common with big dogs, because big dogs need big crates, and big crates are a nuisance. It is worth being patient over this. Remember that this phase does not last forever, but many dogs will need to be in a crate until around their first birthday. Some mouthy dogs – many Labradors and other gun-dog breeds fall into this group – may need crating for another six months or so after this. In the meantime, take comfort in the fact that a dog in a crate cannot empty your bin, destroy your furniture or electrocute himself. It is really that simple.

Another place where dogs can be very destructive is in a vehicle. A small dog can do an incredible amount of damage to the interior of a nice car in the space of ten minutes. Be kind to your car and use a crate!

🐾 In the garden

Puppies love gardening, and digging and pruning figure high on the list of their favourite horticultural activities. You may be reading this because your puppy is wrecking your garden and you are hoping for a solution. If your puppy fancies himself as a landscape gardener, take heart. Most dogs grow out of the urge to dig themselves silly around the same time as they grow out of chewing. In a year or so, your young dog will be happy to sleep among the pots of petunias on your patio, instead of emptying the contents all over it. But for this year at least, you would be well advised to remove anything with soil in it from his reach, and if you have not set up a puppy playpen outdoors, you will need to protect your precious vegetable garden from his attentions using some kind of fence.

This puppy has been left unsupervised on the patio.

Be pro-active

The answer to destructive behaviour is restriction and redirection. Trying to train a nine-week-old puppy not to touch things is futile. Restrict your puppy's access to your precious things, and redirect his natural behaviours to more appropriate items, such as Kongs and other toys. It is annoying to have to take so many steps to stop your puppy getting into mischief and wrecking your home, but in truth it makes for a much quieter life than going into battle with him on a daily basis. If you haven't already, take a look at the final chapter in Part One. It gives you lots of ideas for puppy-proofing your home and garden, and it really is worth the effort.

SUMMARY

- Don't punish your puppy for chewing – it's normal and necessary behaviour.
- Keep items you don't want him to chew out of his reach.
- Most chew toys, except Kongs, need supervision.
- Put your puppy in his crate when you can't keep an eye on him.
- Don't de-crate your puppy at night much before his first birthday.

23

Horrible habits

We may often think of our dogs as family members or close friends, but there are times when they remind us, in no uncertain terms, that they are dogs, through and through. And dogs, it must be said, have some very unpleasant habits.

Eating poo

New puppy owners are sometimes shocked to discover that their beautiful new puppy has developed a taste for consuming his own faeces. Eating poo, also known as coprophagia, is so common among puppies as to be considered fairly normal by experienced breeders, but that is no comfort to you if your puppy likes to indulge. Not only may your puppy be enthusiastic about recycling his own lunch, he may also show an enthusiasm for tucking in to the parcels left by other dogs.

Why do they do it?

We don't know exactly why some dogs eat their own faeces and the faeces of other dogs, although there are plenty of theories. One reason, of course, is simply that the dog likes the taste. Another is that recycling the waste products from his meal gives him a chance to extract every last drop of nutrition from what he is eating.

A study was carried out into this fascinating topic by Dr Benjamin Hart DVM and presented to the 2012 annual symposium of the American Veterinary Society of Animal Behaviour. He found that a significant proportion (16 per cent) of dogs are serious poo eaters. Interestingly, the study also notes that bitches

Poo eating is quite common in puppies.

are more likely to be poo eaters than male dogs. This has been my experience. There are breed differences, too. For example, none of the Poodles in the study ate stools, but 38 per cent of Collies did. I have found it to be a common habit in Labradors.

What we do know is that coprophagia is not restricted to dogs that are starving, under-exercised, bored or otherwise neglected. The best-kept dogs can be members of the coprophagia club, much to the embarrassment of their owners.

Will it harm him?

Once you have got over the shock of his new behaviour, you may well be worried that your puppy will make himself ill. After all, we know that there are all kinds of pathogens in faeces. However, puppies and older dogs don't seem to suffer any ill effects from coprophagia at all.

Once you have been reassured that your puppy is not emotionally disturbed and is unlikely to get sick from his new-found pastime, the next question on your mind will be, 'How do we stop him?' And this is the tricky part.

How do we stop him?

I'm afraid there is no straightforward, cut and dried cure that works for every dog. Some people have claimed complete success in curing coprophagia through adding or subtracting substances from their dogs' diets. We'll have a look at these in a moment. Most of us find the best results are achieved with a combination of behavioural and management strategies. These include:

- Removing temptation
- Supervising when hungry
- Behavioural training

Removing temptation

Many dogs will indulge in coprophagia from time to time. This habit is more likely to form if the dog is exposed to temptation. It may seem obvious, but your dog is less likely to develop a coprophagia habit if you are very committed to clearing up his faeces the second he has emptied himself. Puppies that are allowed unsupervised access to parts of the garden for longish periods of time are more likely to experiment with eating poo. And if they do it, they are likely to enjoy it and want to repeat the experience. The smaller the space that the puppy has access to outdoors, the more likely he is to interact with his own waste products, so this too may be a factor. Clearing up religiously after your puppy can be enough, in some cases, to break the habit completely.

Supervising when hungry

Whilst there is no suggestion that poop eaters are not well fed, I have noticed that dogs with this tendency are more likely to do it when they have an empty tummy, and less likely to indulge when they are full. Focusing your efforts on supervising your puppy when he is hungry, on his first trip outside before breakfast for example, may be more effective than trying to spread your attentions out across the entire day. The reason for supervising the puppy is not just to prevent him scoffing his bowel movements, but also so that you can begin a programme of behaviour modification.

Behavioural training

Modifying your puppy's horrible habit means offering him a better reward for ignoring the object of his desires than the one he is helping himself to. To do this, you will need to choose a chirpy and pleasant signal and associate it with a very nice reward indeed. Then you produce this reward with a flourish in response to changes in your dog's behaviour. Let's have a closer look.

Training your puppy to leave poo on the ground

It may be a less than charming topic, but we have to be specific here. Training is far more successful if we teach dogs what we want them to do, rather than what we don't want them to do.

'Don't eat your poo' is a negative aim. When we have the thought 'don't' in our heads, we tend to look for ways to punish the dog when he does what we don't want him to do. Most of the time, you won't catch the dog in the act so he will get a nice intermittent reward (a yummy snack) for indulging in his behaviour.

What we *want* the puppy to do is leave the poo alone, and we can teach this, with a bit of effort and some great rewards. Here's how.

Step one

Choose a signal. It can be anything you like. A random word, such as 'hooray' or 'brilliant', is fine. Choose something with a happy ring to it, because your natural impulse when you see your dog eating what has just come out of his bottom is to strangle him. Using a nice happy word helps you to stay calm and jolly.

Step two

Associate your signal with some fantastic rewards – roast chicken, chunks of liver sausage, cubes of cheese, whatever floats your dog's boat. Don't try to interrupt poo eating yet. Several times a day say 'hooray' in your chirpiest happy voice and throw the dog a lovely treat.

Step three

Wait until you spot your dog eating poo, or even better just about to eat poo, and give your happy signal 'hooray'. Warning: when you first start to do this, your dog may well scoff down the poo and then come to get his reward. Don't despair. This is because he anticipates you either being angry about the poo, or attempting to take it away. Don't go near the poo! And don't scold the dog. Just reward him as normal.

After a few repetitions of step three you will probably find that the dog will start to leave the poo untouched and rush over for his reward instead. This won't work if you are mean with your rewards, or if you refused to reward him last time because he grabbed the poo and ate it first.

Note: as an interim step, some dogs when they hear your signal will grab the poo and *bring it with them* to get their reward. If the reward is good enough, they will drop the poo in order to get the reward. Throw the reward away from you so they do not see you disposing of the poo.

Dietary strategies

Some people swear by one of a number of additives that you can put in a puppy's food, which supposedly make his poo taste less attractive to him. I have no personal experience of these, but I do know that many people try them with no success. The most popular suggestion seems to be pineapple.

This won't help prevent your puppy from eating what other dogs leave behind, but if done early enough and if it works, it could be sufficient to break the habit. Some people try adding hot or spicy products (chilli pepper for example) to the poo after the puppy has relieved himself, but I suspect they would be better off picking up the poo instead. In any case, many poo eaters tuck in while the snack is still warm.

One dietary strategy that some people say is successful is changing the dog to a raw meat and bones diet. Nowadays, most dogs are fed kibble, which contains a number of additives to make the food palatable. After all, no food manufacturer wants your dog to turn up his nose at their product. So, tasty is the key – tasty enough to still be flavoursome after passing through the dog. Kibble also contains quite a lot of fillers so that the kibble-fed dog's faeces are both bulkier and more strongly flavoured.

A raw-meat diet is digested much more completely and the resulting faeces are largely odourless. Presumably, it doesn't taste as strong either. Most of my own affected dogs left coprophagia behind when I moved them on to a raw diet, although it does return from time to time when I am using a lot of training treats.

According to the study by Ben Hart, based on questioning dog owners, diet did *not* play a part. However, the vast majority of dogs are fed on kibble. Whether there were sufficient numbers of fully raw-fed dogs in the study to make assumptions on this factor is not clear.

Pretty as a picture, but what did she have for lunch?

More horrible habits

Eating poo is not the only horrible habit your puppy may develop. Once he is out and about in the countryside he may discover all sorts of delicious treats, from horse manure and rabbit droppings to human waste and carrion. Some dogs will put themselves at risk by eating plastic wrappers and poisonous mushrooms among other things.

Stopping your dog consuming the discarded contents of a nappy or munching up the remains of a dead seagull can really put a damper on a day at the seaside. So what can you do to make sure this doesn't happen to you? There are no guarantees, but your two weapons are behavioural modification (your magical 'hooray') and physical barriers.

No one wants to put a muzzle on his or her puppy. However, once this type of behaviour is established you may be reduced to muzzling your dog in order to prevent it. Prevention is often more effective than attempting a cure, and started early enough, you may have some success with an extension of the behaviour-modification technique outlined on the previous page.

Make sure you save your magic word 'hooray' for those times when you have an amazing treat to give your dog. Build a really good association with this word for your dog, and you may find you can distract him away from something unpleasant outdoors when the time comes.

You will also benefit from teaching your puppy to recall away from other items and objects that he wants. Place some strong smelling treats up on a high surface, let him see and smell them, but be unable to reach them. Now practise calling your dog away from the temptation. When you are successful, reward him by feeding him a treat from the bowl. The message you are giving him is that the best way to get what he wants lies in seeking your help. You can teach this concept outdoors, too, using a long line to prevent the dog helping himself to his reward. Only when he comes to you for help do you give him what he wants.

Moving away from something he wants in order to receive it is an alien concept for a dog, but it is something that I cover in greater detail in my book *Total Recall*. Essentially, you are teaching your dog that you are the provider of the best rewards, which is half the battle in overcoming this and many other training and behavioural issues.

SUMMARY
- Eating poo is not abnormal or harmful.
- Use a key word and treats to help modify his behaviour.
- Teach your puppy that the best rewards come from you.

24

Guarding food

Your worst fears may be confirmed one day when you approach your puppy's food bowl and he snarls at you. There is no mistaking his intent, he means business. Your puppy stiffens his body and lifts the corner of his lip as he continues to threaten you and growl. All traces of puppy loveliness are gone. Your beautiful friend has been replaced by a monster.

Don't panic! Guarding food is very common, and it does not mean that your puppy is trying to dominate you, or that he has a terrible temperament. In a wild-dog family, as puppies grew bigger, any puppy that did not protect his dinner when resources were tight might starve. So each puppy would grab a little part of the food available and growl at other puppies that try to take it. Of course, domesticated puppies don't normally need to guard their food in this way. But growling over food is an instinctive behaviour that is still present in many puppies today. Some puppies will guard other resources, too, such as toys and bedding, but guarding food is very common indeed.

Dealing with growling

When a puppy growls at us, our natural response is to take away the thing that is causing him to growl. You may well feel that he has no right to guard his food and should not be allowed to do so. Punishing the puppy is also a natural response and may initially seem to work. You have probably seen television shows where growling dogs are punished and/or intimidated into submission in a very short space of time. Unfortunately, these apparently quick fixes may have disastrous long-term results. The puppy or older dog is certainly learning a lesson. He is learning that people approaching his food bowl are a real threat and may steal his food. Worse still, a person approaching his bowl may decide to attack him even when he has taken the trouble to give them a polite warning to back off! Most importantly, the dog is learning that he must *never* growl at people to let them know that he feels threatened by them.

Growling is a *very* important behaviour in a domestic dog. Growling keeps us safe. All dogs have powerful jaws and can deliver a painful and serious bite. When larger dogs bite, the results can be devastating. Growling *precedes a bite* in all normal healthy dogs. It says, 'This is your warning. I feel threatened so back off or I may bite you.' Teaching a dog not to growl before he bites makes him potentially very dangerous indeed. The end result of using punishment on a food-guarding dog is a dog that fears having people near his bowl, and one that may bite *without any warning* at all. His next victim could be a small child who accidentally brushes past him while he is eating, or a visitor who thinks he is happy to be stroked while he tucks into his dinner because the all-important warning growl is absent. Fortunately, there is a better, and permanent, way to cure the problem.

🐾 Curing food guarding

I am going to take you through a structured process to teach a puppy that people approaching his bowl are no threat to him whatsoever. On the contrary, he will learn that people who enter the proximity of his dining area are highly likely to be bringing more food! He will view you as a waiter, rather than a thief. What could be nicer?

By the end of this process you, or anyone else, will be able to put your hands in the puppy's bowl while he is eating, pick up the bowl and touch the puppy while he remains happy and confident throughout. Here are the steps you need to work through. Don't move on to the next step until you have eliminated all growling and *fear* at the previous one. Break the puppy's daily food allowance into as many small meals as you can – the more you practise, the faster he will learn. Completing each step may take two to four days, and longer with older puppies. Be patient – it takes as long as it takes. This is a permanent cure, and well worth the effort.

Exercise one: stand and throw

In this exercise you are going to stand far enough away from your eating puppy so that he feels safe, and throw food towards his bowl. Have a bag of very tasty treats (chunks of roast chicken are ideal) close to hand, or in a treat bag clipped to your belt, and prepare your puppy's meal.

1. Place your puppy's bowl of food in front of him and withdraw to a distance he is comfortable with. He should be relaxed and not growling.
2. Stand still.
3. Start throwing treats towards his bowl while he is eating.
4. Get as many treats into his bowl as you can before he finishes his meal.
5. When he has finished eating, throw a treat well away from his bowl and pick up the bowl while he is looking for the treat.

Don't worry if you miss the bowl – just throw the food in his general direction. It is your intention we want to convey. This is not a demonstration of your throwing skills. Over the next few meal-times, gradually reduce the distance between you and the puppy. Make sure he is comfortable with this. If he growls, or even just stiffens his body, he is not comfortable and you need to back farther away. If you have been in conflict for a while over mealtimes, this may take a little longer than if the problem has only just arisen. When the puppy is happy for you to stand a yard away, switch from

Stand quite still initially – the puppy needs to feel comfortable.

throwing tasty treats to throwing pieces of his dinner (put half in his bowl and the other half in your treat bag). You have completed this stage when you can stand just a yard away from your puppy without him growling while you throw pieces of his dinner into his bowl.

Exercise two: walk and throw

Up until now you have been standing still because this is less threatening to the puppy than you moving about. Once you start to move around him, he may suspect you are going to take his bowl, and may well start to growl again, so you will need to withdraw to a distance where he is comfortable. Start this exercise at about two yards from the puppy, and have some very tasty treats ready. Don't attempt this with his ordinary food to begin with.

1. Place your puppy's bowl of food in front of him, withdraw to a distance he is comfortable with and a bit farther.
2. Start throwing treats towards his bowl while he is eating.
3. Begin to move around him, continuing to throw treats as you do so.
4. Get as many treats into his bowl as you can before he finishes his meal.
5. When he has finished eating, throw a treat well away from his bowl and pick up the bowl while he is looking for the treat.

If your puppy starts to growl, or stiffen, do whatever you have to do to make him feel comfortable again. You can reduce your movements to very small ones, and/or move farther away. Over the next few mealtimes, increase the amount that you walk about, make your movements more pronounced and gradually move closer to the puppy. Your aim is to be able to walk all around the puppy, keeping a distance of about one yard between you. When you can do this, begin talking to the puppy while he is eating and while you throw. When he starts to relax and wag his tail, praise him and tell him how clever he is. Now you can switch back to throwing a proportion of his ordinary food into his bowl. When you get to the stage where your puppy continues to wag his tail while you talk to him and move around him, you are ready to move on to exercise three.

Exercise three: the first touch

The next step is a big one. Your objective is to touch your puppy while he is eating, without him being upset or worried. Don't put your hand anywhere near his mouth or bowl. You can lightly touch his rump or flank, but only when he is ready. Switch back to very tasty treats again. We want this to be a great experience for your dog.

1. Place your puppy's bowl of food in front of him, and remain standing next to him.
2. Start dropping treats into his bowl while he is eating.
3. Brush your hand lightly against his side or back, and throw him a juicy treat.
4. Repeat, getting as many treats into his bowl as you can before he finishes his meal.

5. When he has finished eating, throw a treat well away from his bowl and pick up the bowl while he is looking for the treat.

You need to watch your dog very carefully during this process. He should be happy, relaxed, tail wagging, throughout. If he stiffens his body, move away a bit until he relaxes. You can try again at the next mealtime. It is very important that you go at the dog's pace. Once he is happy and comfortable with you lightly brushing against him, you can move on to firmer but gentle strokes, and eventually to pats. When he is completely relaxed with this, change back to throwing ordinary food in his bowl for a few sessions. Now you are ready to move on to exercise four.

Exercise four: touch with confidence

In this exercise, your objective is to be able to touch your dog's head while he is eating, without him being upset in any way at all. Start with tasty treats as usual.

1. Place your puppy's bowl of food in front of him, and remain standing next to him.
2. Drop a treat into his bowl while he is eating.
3. Brush your hand lightly against his neck and drop another treat into his bowl.
4. If he remains happy, gently stroke his neck and the top of his head while dropping treats into the bowl.
5. If he remains happy, gently stroke his ears while dropping treats into the bowl.
6. Get as many treats into his bowl as you can before he finishes his meal.
7. When he has finished eating, throw a treat well away from his bowl and pick up the bowl while he is looking for the treat.

Eventually he will be happy to be stroked whilst eating.

Remember, an unhappy puppy will stiffen his posture; a happy puppy will be relaxed and wagging his tail when you speak or touch him. If at any point the dog seems unhappy, go back to the previous exercise for a few meals. If he remains relaxed, you can proceed to handle and stroke the dog just as you normally would if he were not eating. But don't touch his bowl or mouth just yet. When he is completely happy to accept normal touches and strokes anywhere else on his body, practise with normal food before moving on to the next exercise.

Exercise five: trust in you

By the end of this exercise your dog will trust you absolutely with his food. He will accept you touching his bowl and even lifting it up, and will remain completely confident that this is not a threat to him in any way. You may need to spread the following steps *over several sessions*. For example, he might be happy with steps one to three, but begin to stiffen up when you attempt step four. Always back up to a point at which the dog is comfortable.

1. Place your puppy's bowl of food in front of him, and remain standing next to him.
2. Drop a treat into his bowl while he is eating.
3. Lower your hand closer to his bowl and drop another treat into it.
4. If he remains happy, move your hand right on to the edge of his bowl and place a treat into it.
5. If he remains happy, put your hand into the bowl and push the treat in among his food.
6. If he remains happy, lift one edge of his bowl, then put a treat in it as you lower the bowl back to the ground.
7. If he remains happy, lift the bowl an inch or two above the ground, then immediately replace it and add a treat.
8. Get as many treats into his bowl as you can before he finishes his meal.
9. When he has finished eating, throw a treat well away from his bowl and pick up the bowl while he is looking for the treat.

Continue to practise and work on touching the dog all around his mouth and face, patting him quite firmly and ruffling his ears as a child or visitor might. Practise lifting the bowl higher, until you can place it on a work surface. Always return the bowl to the dog immediately and making sure you add tasty treats to it. Remember to congratulate yourself for getting to this point. You have done an amazing job and your dog now trusts you 100 per cent with his food. The final lesson to teach him is that other people are as well intentioned as you are.

Exercise six: trust in everyone

This final exercise is actually a series of exercises. Ask other members of your family, or friends and neighbours, to work through the same exercises. Don't worry, it won't take them as long as it took you. The biggest hurdle has been achieved and your dog now simply needs to be reassured that people in general are not interested in stealing his food.

This process may seem like a very big deal because I have included sufficient steps to cope with the most fearful of puppies. Many of you will find the process far simpler than it looks when written down.

Your confident puppy

During this whole procedure, especially with young puppies, you may find the dog quickly loses all his anxiety and forgets to guard his bowl at all, even to the point of leaving the bowl and repeatedly approaching you and anyone else nearby to beg for treats. This is ideal. However, it is important to remain aware of warning signs. Observe your puppy very carefully at all times. Stop and back up if he seems unhappy, or if he stops eating and stiffens his body.

Once you have achieved your goal, don't keep testing your dog by taking his dinner away constantly, and when you do remove his bowl, it should always be to add something nice to it. You want him to believe that anyone anywhere near his bowl is a very good thing.

Remember, never touch or punish an angry growling puppy. You might get bitten, and even if you make your puppy too afraid to bite *you*, he may still bite other people. Food guarding is wonderfully straightforward to cure in young puppies. Just follow the steps in this chapter and your puppy will soon be happy to have people around him while he is eating.

> ## SUMMARY
> - Never punish your puppy for growling at you.
> - Teach him he can trust people with his food in several stages.
> - Always put something tasty in his bowl when you return it to him.

25
Switching to raw feeding

Most puppy owners choose to feed kibble for at least the first few months, but if you have made up your mind to have a go at raw feeding, this chapter is for you. It can be a daunting and somewhat lonely business, feeding a completely raw diet to a young puppy, especially if your vet disapproves and you don't know anyone else who is feeding raw food to their dogs. However, raw feeding is no more complicated than feeding a sensible diet to your growing children, and most us manage to do that successfully.

If you are undecided whether or not to feed raw, or don't really know what is involved, or what the benefits and risks are, please do read Chapter 5, 'Feeding your puppy', before making up your mind.

You will need a good-sized freezer with plenty of space in it, because you may need to order several weeks' food at once. If you don't already have one, you will need a large chopping board dedicated to raw meat and some sharp butcher's knives. A mallet or hammer to break bones can also be useful. If you are going to take advantage of opportunistic finds that come your way, such as offcuts from your butcher, or a few rabbits shot by a friend, or part of the catch after a day's fishing, then you will need freezer bags and labels to pack and store what you don't use that day.

What can I feed to my puppy?

The method of raw feeding described in this chapter is sometimes referred to as the whole prey model. That is to say, the dog is fed raw meat, bone and organs in similar proportions to those that you find in a typical animal. The term 'prey model' should not be taken too literally, but should rather encourage you to make sure your dog gets a variety of different body parts, with enough muscle meat in proportion to bone, as well as different types of animal. It is tempting to rely on foods that are easily available, and many people who feed raw to their dogs depend predominantly on chicken, especially chicken backs and other items discarded from the human food chain. Be aware that these can sometimes be very bony, and don't rely on them too heavily. It is important that your dog has a range of different types of meat, including fish and eggs, in order to give him all the nutrients he needs. This is particularly important with puppies under six months of age.

Fish are an important source of food for raw-fed dogs, and small ones can be fed whole so that the dog can benefit from the range of nutrients found in organs, including the eyes and brain. All dogs seem to have the instinctive knowledge to turn a fish around and swallow it head first, thus avoiding being prickled by the fins, but I do snip the fins off any fish with very sharp spines. You may need to take the heads off larger fish, as the preponderance of small bones seems to make many dogs sick. Green tripe smells terrible, but it contains important nutrients and should be fed once or twice every week.

You don't need to feed every nutrient your dog needs, every day. Just like people, provided the nutrient deficit does not last too long, dogs are able to utilise nutrients when they are available and cope when they are not. Aim to give your dog a full range of nutrients over the space of a few days. He will need muscle, bone, organs (including heart and lungs), connective tissue and fat. Make sure young puppies get some bone and eggs most days, and fish a couple of times a week.

Here are some examples of raw meat that can be fed to a dog:

- Fresh fish (take heads off the really big ones)
- Chicken, turkey (including backs, feet and wings)
- Rabbits (whole, with or without skin)
- Eggs
- Lamb, venison, pork or beef ribs
- Pig's trotters or heads (split open)
- Heart, lungs and very small quantities of liver from herbivores
- Green tripe (lamb or beef)

Where do I buy raw food for my puppy?

You will need to find an affordable supplier of raw meat and fish *on the bone*. Sometimes a local butcher will be able to offer you cheap offcuts, but they are catching on now to the increase in raw feeding and good deals are harder to find. Some large pet shops sell a range of frozen raw food. There are also a number of companies dedicated to supplying the raw dog-food market. You can find them and order from them online. Many will do monthly deliveries only as they cover large areas, which is why you need a good-sized freezer.

The question of bone

Too little bone in a raw diet is likely to cause very loose stools, and to deprive the dog of important nutrients, which is particularly relevant when it comes to puppies. They need adequate nutrients for growth and to avoid developing rickets.

On the other hand, *too much* bone may cause problems, too. Exactly how much is too much has not been established in tests and trials. All we have to go on is what experienced raw feeders are feeding their dogs without problems. Many raw-feeding websites advocate, as a rough guide, that 10 per cent of your dog's diet should be bone. My dogs probably eat quite a bit more bone than this, but they are experienced raw eaters. The concern, if bone content rises too high, is that the dog may become severely constipated and could even suffer from a gastrointestinal blockage. Vets will tell you that they occasionally see a dog with impacted bowel contents. Usually this responds to plenty of fluids and/or an enema. In severe cases, an operation may be required to empty the bowel and clear the blockage. Whether these cases are arising in dogs fed bone as part of a balanced raw diet is not clear, but some experts feel that recreational bones are more likely to be the culprit.

Recreational bones

A recreational bone is one that is given to the dog to entertain him and is not part of a meal or accompanied by generous quantities of muscle meat and other tissues. The dog chips away quietly at the recreational bone over the course of an hour or so and swallows quite a lot of fragments. Many dogs seem to be able to cope with these bones without problems, but some clearly do not.

It is possible that the dog's ability to process bone develops the longer he is on a raw diet. Too much bone too soon may possibly increase the risk of impacted bone collecting in the dog's bowels, causing constipation. This seems a reasonable assumption and a sensible approach to increasing the proportion of bone in a dog's diet is to do so gradually.

The more bone your dog has eaten, the more he will want to drink. Make sure your dog has access to clean drinking water at all times, but *especially* an hour or so after eating a meal with a high proportion of bone.

Gulpers

Some puppies gulp down their food so quickly that they don't break up the bone properly first. This can be dangerous. Chicken wings are great food for puppies, but if your puppy is a gulper and tries to down the wing in one go, you will need to smash each wing a couple of times with your mallet before giving it to him. Signs that your puppy is swallowing bones that are too large for him to cope with are a) difficulty swallowing his food, and b) pieces of bone in his stools.

If you are getting this right, you should not see lumps of bone in your puppy's stools, because all the bone will be digested. Standing over puppies or older dogs while they eat can cause gulping in a dog that wouldn't gulp otherwise. This is because the puppy values raw food so highly and is afraid you will take it away.

Regurgitation

Puppies and dogs that are not used to raw food will often regurgitate what they have eaten, and then eat it again, possibly several times. This happens almost immediately after eating and looks quite disgusting, so don't watch. It is not harmful and it won't harm the puppy to eat it up again, which he will almost certainly attempt to do.

Beware of interfering when your puppy regurgitates. If you try to wrestle the mess off him, he may gulp it down too quickly, instead of working on it a bit more to break down the bones.

How much to feed?

Whilst it isn't rocket science, raw feeding does require that you give a little thought to balancing the diet and feeding enough variety. If getting the balance right seems daunting, bear in mind that most of us manage to raise healthy kids without weighing everything they eat, or giving them supplements.

Judge how much to feed by how your puppy looks and feels. As a very rough guide to get you started, we can generalise that a healthy *adult* dog will need around 2–3 per cent of his body weight each day in order to stay in shape. So a 100lb dog would need two to three pounds of raw meat and bone per day, a 50lb dog would need one to one and a half pounds, and a 25lb dog might need half to three-quarters of a pound. Requirements do not increase in direct proportion to size. Big dogs may need to eat a smaller proportion of their body weight than this, whilst smaller dogs may need to eat more than the guideline.

Importantly, you need to know that puppies need even *more* food for their size than adult dogs. This is because we are fuelling the puppy's growth. Therefore, we normally aim to feed around 10 per cent of the puppy's weight per day to begin with. Again this is a very rough guide. Feed according to how your puppy looks and feels, not by the scales.

How to feed it

Allocate a sheltered place outdoors for your puppy to eat, either on a patch of grass or on a hoseable surface. He is going to make quite a mess. Divide your puppy's daily rations into several portions – we normally say, as a rough guide, four portions per day up to three months, three per day up to six months, then two per day until the end of the first year. However, many raw-fed puppies can cope with fewer, larger portions a bit sooner. Your guide is your puppy's appearance and his stools, which should be firm and almost odourless. If stools are loose, feed less and divide it into more helpings. Check to make sure you haven't fed too much liver and are feeding enough bone. If your puppy seems a bit constipated, give him more muscle meat and less bone.

Don't stand over a puppy while he is eating raw meat, and make sure children cannot reach or touch him during or after his meal. Puppies can be very possessive over real food, and if they think you are going to take it back, they will try to swallow it as fast as they can. Hanging around your puppy while he is eating may very well turn him into a gulper. Keep a watchful eye from a distance and let him relax with his food.

After eating raw food, your puppy's mouth and face will be covered with raw-meat juices, so it is a good idea to keep him well away from small children after each meal, and wash your hands very thoroughly after handling him.

What to avoid feeding

I don't feed animals that have died of natural causes or been killed on the roads. This is because animals that get run over may be more likely to have been unhealthy, and animals that have died from unknown causes may have diseases or toxins that could be passed on to the dog. I see no point in taking extra risks. I don't feed very large fish with the heads on because the bones make all my dogs sick, and this can be up to several hours later. It doesn't bother the dog, but it bothers me because I have to clean it up.

Never feed bones that have been cooked, and avoid large weight-bearing bones from big herbivores. A very experienced raw-fed dog may know when he is defeated, but some dogs will strive to break down and swallow these large bones, possibly damaging their teeth in the process.

Getting started

Some raw feeders believe that you should never feed kibble and raw together. The argument behind this advice states that kibble has a different gut transit time from raw food, and that kibble in the gut may delay the digestion of the raw food, reduce the acidity in the stomach, and allow bacteria to proliferate. Some even warn of dire consequences if you mix the two diets. I have not been able to find any research to support these theories.

It won't do any harm if you switch 'cold turkey' and cease to offer any kibble right from the start, provided your puppy is old enough to cope with a low-calorie intake for a day or two. This is because you need to feed very small quantities of raw for the first few days to avoid upsetting your dog's tummy. With small puppies this is problematic, because a small puppy cannot cope with a very reduced quantity of food for very long.

Any kibble-fed puppies that I have purchased, I switch over to raw by introducing a little minced chicken to their kibble, gradually increasing the proportions of meat and reducing the proportions of kibble over the space of a few days. If

Views are divided on the wisdom of mixing kibble and raw food together.

you want to feed raw and kibble separately, you will need to leave a gap of several hours between the two different types of meal.

Once the puppy has had several small meals of chicken mince and is producing nice firm stools, you can begin to add chicken wingtips. Observe your puppy from a distance. Watch to see how he behaves. If he crunches along the length of the wingtip and then swallows it, you are off to a good start. At the next meal you can offer him an entire chicken wing. If he simply swallows the wingtip instantly, you will need your mallet before giving him a whole wing. Take a chicken wing and lay it on a chopping board. Hit it several times with the mallet to break the bone inside into sections. The bone remains wrapped in its meaty muscle parcel, but is less likely to get stuck on the way down, and is easier to digest.

Don't be tempted to cut up your dog's food into small pieces. Cutting up food may increase the risk of choking. It is far better to feed bigger portions so that the puppy has to work at the food and cannot just gulp it down whole.

🐾 Adding variety

After a few days on chicken, you can add some eggs to the puppy's diet. One egg cracked into his bowl to begin with makes a great breakfast for a small puppy. With a larger pup, you can build up to two or three eggs. If all goes well, and your puppy's tummy is still settled, start adding another meat – minced green tripe is a good choice – in tiny quantities to begin with.

Continue in this way, adding *just one* new type of meat or fish every few days. If you make the transition gradually like this, all should go smoothly. If your puppy gets an upset stomach, don't assume it is necessarily his food. Puppies get sick sometimes. Call your vet if you are at all worried. If the problem is a mild one, eliminate the food you suspect and try it again in tiny quantities when the puppy is a bit older. The cause of the upset tummy could be entirely unrelated.

Not a magic wand

A great many people who start to feed a raw diet do so because their dog already has problems that have not been resolved on a diet of kibble. In some cases, these problems may have been erroneously attributed to the kibble itself. Common reasons for switching are digestive problems, behavioural problems and skin allergies. Yet there is currently little, if any, evidence to suggest that a raw diet can cure any of these ailments. This may result in disappointment for those who have pinned their hopes on a better life for their dog.

Switching to raw is not a magic wand. There are no *guarantees* that your dog will appear to be any healthier than he was before, and there are potential risks, which cannot be discounted out of hand. It can be difficult to find objective help and advice for newcomers to raw feeding. Your greatest asset will be a supportive veterinary surgeon, if you can find one, who recognises that kibble has its disadvantages, too, and who is willing to accept that raw feeding is a reasonable and rational choice for a well-informed puppy owner and his pet.

Raw feeding can be both challenging and very rewarding. Some people try it and then decide it isn't for them. Don't worry if this happens to you. On the other hand, if you decide to stick at it, your dog will keep his sparkling white teeth into old age, and you will have the certain daily pleasure of watching him tuck in, with blissful rapture, to the delicious meaty meals that nature intended him to have.

Your puppy will thoroughly enjoy his meaty meals.

SUMMARY

- Don't feed your puppy recreational or cooked bones.
- Do increase bone proportions gradually.
- Don't disturb your dog while he is eating raw food.
- Do keep children away from your dog while he is eating and for some time afterwards.
- Do crush larger bones *within the muscle* for puppies and small dogs.
- Don't cut food up into little chunks.
- Allow your puppy to eat his regurgitated food, if he wants to.
- Take extra care to ensure puppies have sufficient variety.

26

Neutering and sexual maturity

hen I was a child in the 1960s, dogs were not confined and supervised to the extent that they are in the UK today. Our village had its own local population of dogs, many of which were free to roam at will. I remember an elderly Golden Retriever that used to warm his old bones by sleeping in the road so that all the cars had to drive around him; and a terrier that would rush out of its gate and make you jump as you walked down the road.

In those days, genuinely stray dogs were a big problem and neutering was an important part of controlling the local dog population. Historically, vets supported and promoted this use of neutering as a form of birth control. It has to be said that there are less invasive forms of birth control available for modern dogs, including the sensible management of your pet. This is a fairly

You don't need to decide quite yet.

straightforward matter nowadays, as most of us do not allow our dogs to roam the streets unattended. But what about the health benefits of neutering? Is your dog likely to be healthier, better behaved or live longer if you separate him from his gonads? Not so long ago, experts would have answered, almost unanimously, 'yes'. However, a lot more research has been undertaken since then, and now the situation is altogether less clear.

Before we look at the information currently available to us, let's have a look at what is involved in neutering your pet, and at what is involved in keeping a sexually mature dog or bitch.

Having your bitch spayed

Having a female dog neutered is a major procedure. The vet will administer a general anaesthetic and make an incision in her belly. He will then remove her uterus and ovaries before stitching her up. It will be a few days before she feels herself and a couple of weeks before she is back to normal. The cost of this operation will probably not be covered by your insurance and can amount to a considerable sum.

Some people have their bitches spayed as a matter of convenience. An unspayed bitch will normally come into season twice a year. Each season lasts for around three weeks and during this time she will have a bloody vaginal discharge and be attractive to male dogs. Some bitches keep themselves very clean at this time; others are less fastidious and need to be kept on washable floors for the duration. This process usually starts towards the end of the first year but can begin at any time from around the age of six months.

Some bitches show mild behavioural changes when they are in season. They may be more clingy, and can be grumpy with other bitches. Your bitch will want to wee a lot more when she is on heat and may even have the odd accident in the house. Having said that, most bitches go through each season with very little effect on the rest of the family.

Dogs of both sexes can be remarkably inventive about getting up close and personal while bitches are on heat, overcoming all manner of barriers and differences in size. You will need to be very sure that your bitch is not accessible to other dogs in order to avoid an unwanted pregnancy. This may include restricting her walks during this time.

🐾 Having your dog castrated

This is a somewhat simpler operation. The dog's testicles are removed through a small incision, and he will be back to normal within a day or two. After a period of time, the operation will render him completely infertile. It will also deprive him of his main source of the male hormone testosterone. Your dog will be less interested in bitches in season, and therefore less likely to try to escape from a poorly fenced garden in order to roam the streets looking for sex. If you intend to exercise your dog in popular public places, you will meet people daft enough to take a bitch on heat out in public. This will not normally bother a castrated dog.

Castrating your puppy may decrease the chances of him being aggressive towards other male dogs in the future, although it must be said that many intact male dogs also remain perfectly friendly throughout their lives and do not get involved in regular punch-ups as a result of their hormones.

Deciding whether or not to neuter this little pug is not an easy matter.

A common misconception is that neutering will dramatically alter your dog's temperament and make him or her calmer. You should be aware that castrating your male puppy will *not* stop him being boisterous and bouncy. It won't stop him jumping up, dragging you around on the end of the lead or digging up your flowerbeds. It will not cure bad manners of any kind, nor will it necessarily make your male Dog more trainable. Roaming can be prevented by proper fencing and supervision, and some castrated dogs will *still roam* if not properly supervised.

Studies suggest that testosterone makes dogs more reactive, so that an aggressive dog may react more intensely and for longer to a threat. But castrating a dog does not necessarily prevent aggression from occurring in the first place. In fact, some vets feel that a sensitive or nervous dog is *less* likely to be fearful (and therefore aggressive) if left intact, as testosterone is a confidence-boosting hormone. For that reason, some vets will recommend that such a dog is left in possession of his testicles.

🐾 Are there health benefits to neutering?

There are some important health benefits to spaying your bitch. The most clear-cut is the prevention of pyometra, a potentially fatal infection of the uterus (womb), which swells dramatically as it fills with pus. When pyometra occurs, it tends to develop within a few weeks of the bitch having completed her season. It can be difficult to spot, because the symptoms can be vague until the infection is advanced. Treatment is usually an emergency spay, which is riskier and more expensive than elective surgery. Many dog owners are not aware of pyometra, and of those who are, most are unaware of just how common it is. One American study put the risk at 66 per cent in bitches over nine years old. In other words, your female puppy is more likely to get pyometra than not, and the chances of her developing this condition increase with every year as she ages. Spaying removes this risk almost entirely.

Early spaying has been shown to reduce the risk of mammary cancer, provided it is carried out before the second season. It is doubtful if much protection is afforded to bitches that are spayed after this time. Very early spaying (before the first season) is believed to eliminate the risk of mammary cancer almost entirely. The risk of cancer in an unspayed bitch may depend partly on which breed she is. If you own a breed at higher than average risk for cancer, this may influence your decision and is something to discuss with your vet.

A recent American study of over 40,000 dogs has shown that neutered dogs live around a year and a half longer than intact dogs. On closer inspection, however, it becomes clear that the two groups of dogs in the study (neutered and intact) died from somewhat different causes.

The spayed and castrated dogs were more likely to die from autoimmune diseases and cancer, whilst the intact dogs were more likely to die from infectious disease and trauma. One explanation for these statistics is that the intact dogs were more likely to have roamed or, in a society where neutering is considered the duty of responsible owners, to have received less care and attention from their owners. Another explanation could be that neutering in some way improves the dog's ability to fight disease. It isn't clear which of these factors came in to play and to what extent. What we do know is that infectious disease and trauma are significantly under the control of the dog's owner, through adequate vaccination and supervision. It would be interesting to compare the lifespan of these two groups of dogs if both received the same care and supervision. Otherwise, it is perhaps inappropriate to conclude from this study that removing your dog's reproductive equipment is definitely going to give him a longer, or healthier, life.

What about disadvantages?

Spaying interferes with your bitch's hormones, and this can, after a period of time, result in incontinence. This may be more of a problem in bitches that are spayed very young, and in many cases this type of incontinence can be adequately treated with tablets.

It has been claimed that cranial cruciate ligament ruptures are more common in neutered dogs, which might be a consideration if you intend to compete with your dog in a physical sport, such as agility. Other studies have shown that castration will make your male dog *less* susceptible to some cancers and *more*

Easy neutering will protect this beautiful puppy from certain diseases, but what are the downsides?

susceptible to others. More studies on this subject are coming out all the time. Check the references at the back of this book for more information, and ask your vet for his opinion on the latest research.

Other effects of neutering

Sex hormones influence growth, and neutering can lengthen the growth period in your puppy, resulting in a taller dog. Early castration may also have a slightly feminising effect on the appearance of a male dog.

Spaying a bitch may have a significant effect on her coat, which needs to be taken into consideration if you want to show your dog. My recently spayed Cocker Spaniel bitch has lost her glossy coat and now resembles a badly made hearthrug. This is a normal side effect of spaying. It doesn't bother me, but it might upset you.

Whether or not you decide to have your dog neutered is a very personal decision. Be wary of a vet who paints too rosy a picture of the deed, is not interested in discussing the latest research on this important topic, or who is not willing to discuss the disadvantages of neutering. Neutering may well be the right course of action for you, particularly if your dog is female, but being fully informed is really the best and only way to make the right choice.

SUMMARY
- Neutering will not alter your puppy's character.
- Neutering has health benefits, especially for bitches.
- Weigh up the advantages and disadvantages before deciding whether your puppy should be neutered or not.

27
The disobedient puppy

Disobedience can rear its ugly head at any time, but it is common for it to make its first appearance at around three to four months. This tiny puppy is clearly very smart. He has learned to sit, stay and shake paws within two weeks of taking up residence in your home. Then, when he is fourteen or fifteen weeks old, he starts just ignoring you. Puppy owners the world over recognise the signs, and often report episodes of 'deliberate naughtiness' and may describe their puppy's behaviour as 'wilful' or 'dominant'. Another common time for a puppy to begin to defy his owner, especially outdoors, is at the point of emerging independence. This is often between six and nine months of age. So what makes a previously well-behaved puppy start to defy his owner, and what can you do about it? Let's take a closer look at what defines a disobedient dog.

Deliberate naughtiness?

All dog owners have done it – spent several days perfecting a piece of 'dog training' and then, bursting with pride, announced a demonstration of prowess to a loved one or friend. 'Rover. Fetch,' you command, as you wave an imperious finger towards his favourite ball, upon which Rover looks you squarely in the eye and very carefully lies down and rolls on his back. Dogs have a habit of embarrassing you whenever you try to demonstrate a newly learned skill. We'll look at why that is in a moment, because the natural assumption is that they are doing it on purpose.

I think most of us would agree that disobedience is a refusal to obey a known command or instruction. A dog that has been taught to come when he is called

She won't respond when playing with another dog; this is a skill she needs to be taught.

is surely being disobedient if he refuses to obey your recall whistle when another dog wants to play with him.

'My dog knows what to do but just defies me,' or words to that effect, is perhaps the most common complaint about disobedience that I have come across. The owner is convinced that her dog 'knows what to do' because for days, if not weeks, he was doing everything she asked him to. Not unreasonably, the frustrated dog owner concludes that the dog is deliberately defying her. A dog that knows what to do and then fails to do it is being disobedient, right?

Well, not really, and I will explain why. There are two factors we may need to take into account when observing a failure to comply with our perfectly reasonable requests. One is the maturity of the puppy, and the other is the ability, or lack thereof, of dogs to generalise information.

Your puppy's attention span

Puppies, like young children, have short attention spans. When we teach a puppy a new skill, such as sit, we often add some duration and difficulty to that skill very rapidly. It is exciting to see just how quickly puppies learn and we tend to compete with ourselves to see how much more we can do today than we did the day before. Your puppy sat still for three seconds yesterday, so today you ask for ten seconds, and the next day for twenty. Before you know where you are, you have a ten-week-old puppy sitting still for nearly a minute!

But hold on. This is not going to last. He is just a baby, and sooner rather than later he is going to get bored and wander off. He isn't being naughty; he just lacks the ability to concentrate for more than a few seconds. That is one of the reasons why you will find the lessons in this book broken down into such simple and gradual stages.

I totally empathise with your enthusiasm to train this intelligent and willing little dog, and even to push him to achieve his potential, but it is important to recognise that there is nothing to be gained from 'hot housing' your new friend. He will never have to pass exams, and no one but you will ever care how many commands he knows, or how long he can sit still for. There is also a very real risk that you will jeopardise the nice relationship you are building with your puppy, and his enthusiasm to be with you, if you push him too hard, too soon.

It is far better that you keep his attention and his enjoyment of the lessons, so that you have a keen and willing pupil for years to come, than make a very young and immature little dog convinced that being with you is about as interesting as watching paint dry.

Any time, any how, anywhere

Puppies, and older dogs, too, lack a skill that humans are quite good at. If you teach your baby to clap his hands in your kitchen, you can then rush around to your neighbour's kitchen and say, 'Look what he can do! Clap your hands for Auntie Sue, Jamie,' and little Jamie will probably give Auntie Sue a beautiful demonstration of his impressive new skill.

So when you teach your puppy to sit on command in your kitchen, and rush around to Auntie Sue to display his brilliance, it is very frustrating to find that he just stands there wagging his little tail and looking at you as though you are demented.

Once we realise the dog's limitations in his ability to generalise a command from one situation to another, it is possible to forgive him for making us look silly. The truth is that a puppy has not the slightest idea that the word sit means the same thing in one place as it means in any other. You have to teach him this through the process we call proofing (see Chapter 20, 'Towards obedience'), and it takes time.

The trained response

We tend to think of obedience as a choice, as it is for humans. We believe that a puppy can choose to defy or obey, and of course we want him to choose to be obedient. But animal training actually does not work this way. What we are creating in a well-trained dog is a series of trained responses, automatic reactions to a signal that the dog hears or sees. That is all it is. A fully trained dog doesn't come rushing joyfully towards you on a busy beach, ignoring all the temptations around him, because he had a little chat with himself about the pros and cons. He doesn't do it because he loves and respects you, or even because he fears you. He comes because it is an automatic response, trained at home where there are no distractions and then proofed over weeks and months in all the likely scenarios in which you and your dog are likely to find yourselves. And yes, eventually, that trained response is so ingrained, so automatic, that the dog is able at last to generalise that your signal applies any time, any how, anywhere.

The beauty of proofing

Proofing is a beautiful process. It opens your puppy's eyes to the extraordinary (to him) possibility that the magical signal, which he loves to respond to at home, is just as magical anywhere else. It is not, however, an easy or quick process and that is why it doesn't make for great television, and has little celebrity appeal. You can't take a wayward dog and transform it in a one-hour TV show. Proofing is not particularly fashionable or cool. It is, however, the only way, successfully and permanently, to teach a dog that sit really does mean sit. You can find out more about this important stage in training, in Chapter 20, 'Towards obedience'.

It is not too late to start over

If you have messed up a bit with your training, and your puppy is being thoroughly disobedient, don't worry about it. All you have messed up is the particular cue or command that you use to trigger a particular behaviour. There are plenty more cues you can choose instead. If you have accidentally taught your puppy that come means 'run around like a lunatic and play with any other dogs in the vicinity', all you messed up is the dog's response to the word 'come', not his ability to recall. You simply need to start over with a new command, such as 'here', and to train properly *in stages*, without rushing, and spend plenty of time on proofing.

It is always a good idea to use a new command if your puppy has been repeatedly ignoring the old one. This is because the puppy has made negative associations with your failed command, which will interfere with your ability to retrain that skill. You can choose a different word, or switch to a hand signal, or a whistle. I like whistles and particularly recommend them for anyone sharing their home with children or other relatives who have a tendency to interfere with the dog's training. If you have a whistle, you can put the whistle away where no one else can use it.

Pre-empting trouble

Many people get into difficulties with obedience outdoors, especially with recall. Avoiding problems is far easier than attempting to cure them, and a thorough programme of training and proofing is the best way forward. In the meantime, one simple rule that helps many dog owners out of doors is to be more interesting to their puppy. Try not to treat a walk as a time when you just switch off while the dog does his own thing. This is a sure way of getting into difficulties. Take a ball with you, change direction often so that your puppy has to keep looking for you, interact with him and reward him often and generously when he checks in. You can find a lot more information on this topic in my book *Total Recall*.

Remember not to train beyond your puppy's understanding. If you have not trained him to recall in the presence of other dogs, don't attempt to recall him

Keep her interested and watching you.

'Did you call? Only I'm a bit busy right now.'

while he is engrossed in the best game ever with your neighbour's poodle. Take it one step at a time. Do your utmost to make each new exercise laughably easy, so that the puppy cannot fail, then gradually increase the level of difficulty until you reach the standard you are aiming for.

'Do this' rather than 'don't do that'

It is worth reminding ourselves from time to time that we need to focus on what we want the puppy to *do*, rather than what we *don't* want him to do. We can usually teach puppies alternatives to bad behaviours. Puppies learn to yap for attention, or to scrabble at doors. We taught them to do the bad thing by giving them attention, or other rewards – opening the door while the puppy is scratching at the paintwork, for example. When puppies do these naughty things, many people's first instinct is to try to figure out how to stop the behaviour. We worry about how we can stop the dog barking, or digging, or stealing the children's toys. Yet we are often more successful in terminating bad behaviour if we shift our focus from the behaviour we do *not* want, to a suitable *alternative*. Instead of trying to stop a dog climbing on the sofa, we can teach him to lie on a mat on the floor. Instead of scolding him for jumping up at visitors, we can teach him to sit as he greets people.

Staying calm

Outdoor disobedience is often linked to inadequate supervision and interaction whereas many of the difficulties that people get into with puppies indoors are closely linked to overexcitement. We talked about some of the problems that can arise when puppies get overexcited during play, but overstimulation and the resulting excitement is also a common cause of bad behaviour generally. Signs of overexcitement include whining, spinning, jumping, panting, yapping, paddling the front feet and so on. It is hard for a puppy to hear and respond to your signals when he is in this kind of state. Calm puppies are happier and easier to manage than hysterical ones, so try to avoid reinforcing excitable behaviour.

Dogs learn very quickly that certain actions we routinely take are predictors of a reward. Your puppy *will* become excited when one of your actions predicts a reward on a regular basis. He sees the lead come off its hook and he knows it means you are about to put his lead on. He spins and barks with excitement while you clip on the lead, reinforcing his bad behaviour. He is now even more excited because he knows that the lead predicts you are about to open the front door, which in turn predicts the start of the walk.

We can resolve these kinds of problems by being less predictable. Get his lead off the hook ten minutes before you intend to go for a walk. If he is overexcited, don't attach the lead. Wait for him to calm down. If he gets excited once the lead is on, don't open the front door. Leave him trailing his lead around the house until he has calmed down. If you have taught your dog to sit to say please, then all you need do is wait for a calm sit before taking the next action in the chain.

It is worth going to some trouble with this kind of behavioural modification while your dog is still a puppy. These things are harder to alter once the habit is deeply ingrained.

Learning to relax – your space and his space

Some dogs can become quite a nuisance at home in the evenings when the family is trying to relax. It is not uncommon for dogs to poke and pester anyone that sits in a chair, looking constantly for attention and even barking if ignored.

This puppy would love a few minutes alone with these boots.

These behaviours become established because family members have inadvertently rewarded the dog with attention when he pokes at their hands or scrabbles at their legs. Alternatively, the dog may entertain himself by endlessly touching and taking things he should not have, or climbing all over the furniture.

Sharing a home with your dog does not mean you have to allow him to occupy every part of your home, or that he is entitled to your undivided attention from dawn until dusk. In fact, most dogs are much happier if they can learn to relax in your company and to lie by your feet and sleep while you watch television or chat to your friends. It is fine for you to have your own space, rooms where dogs are not allowed. For many people this includes the bedroom or the whole of the upstairs of their home. For some families it includes the living room where family members relax in the evenings. I have a compromise. My dogs are allowed in the living room, but only when they have been taught to lie still. This takes time and effort but it is worth it.

Many of you will want to treat the dog as any other member of the family and give him access to all the rooms in your house. This is fine once he is house-trained and provided he is able to relax in your company and stay out of trouble. But when problems develop, you may need to rescind these privileges for a while. If your dog won't leave you alone while you watch TV, if he steals your cushions or creeps on the sofa uninvited, pop a baby gate across your living-room door and allow him into that room for just a short period each evening while you teach him to lie on a designated mat, cushion or chair. Keep his privileged access to your inner sanctum short until he is reliably able to remain there without making a nuisance of himself, then gradually increase the time he is allowed to remain with you.

A beautiful friendship

It is difficult to put a price on the value of getting off to a good start with your puppy, of not expecting too much, too soon, of keeping him calm, and of establishing a repertoire of simple basic behaviours. A well-mannered dog, trained with consideration and kindness, can relax in the knowledge that he knows what is expected of him, and that his presence is appreciated.

Bringing a dog into your home will change your life forever. You have the power to make it a positive change. Try to remember that puppies have no concept of right or wrong, or of good or bad. Difficult puppies are not wilful or naughty; they simply do what has worked for them in the past. This gives you both control and responsibility, because a disobedient puppy is, in truth, incapable of responding *at that moment in time.* Whether this is because he is too excited to communicate with you, or because you have not proofed that particular command is for you to decide. But the answer lies in your hands, not his.

If you accept that responsibility willingly, and acknowledge your role in educating your puppy gently, and in helping him to become a part of your world, I believe you will enjoy his all too brief babyhood immensely. Your happy puppy will grow into a happy dog, and yours will be a beautiful and enduring friendship.

SUMMARY
- Don't expect too much of your puppy too soon.
- Teaching him that a cue he responds to in one place means the same in another takes time and patience.
- Reinforce calm behaviour and encourage your puppy to relax.
- Interact with your puppy on walks so that he enjoys staying close to you.

Resources

1 A new life

1. **John Bradshaw:** In Defence of Dogs, Penguin Books, 2011
2. **Raymond and Lorna Coppinger:** A New Understanding of Canine Origin, Behaviour and Evolution, Crosskeys Select Books, 2004

2 How puppies learn

1. **American Veterinary Society of Animal Behavior:** Position statement on the use of dominance theory in behaviour modification of animals avsabonline. org/uploads/position_statements/dominance_statement.pdf
2. **Karen Pryor:** Don't Shoot the Dog, Ringpress Books, revised edition, 2002
3. **Meghan E. Herron, Frances S. Shofer, Ilana Reisner:** Survey of the use and outcome of confrontational and non-confrontational training methods in client-owned dogs showing undesirable behaviours vet.osu.edu/assets/pdf/hospital/behaviour/trainingArticle.pdf
4. **E.F. Hiby, N.J. Rooney, J.W.S. Bradshaw:** Dog training methods: their use, effectiveness and interaction with behaviour and welfare, Animal Welfare 13:63-69, 2004
5. **Pamela Reid:** Excel-erated Learning, James and Kenneth Publishers, 1996

3 Raising a friendly puppy

1. **David Appleby (Association of Pet Behaviour Counsellors):** Puppy Socialisation and Habituation (Part One) Why is it necessary? www.apbc.org.uk/articles/puppysocialisation1
2. **Jozsef Topal, Marta Gacsi, Adam Mik-** losi, Zsofia Viranyi, Eniko Kubinyi and Vilmos Csanyi: Attachment to humans: A comparative study on hand-reared wolves and differently socialized dog puppies 2005 www.behav.org/00library/articles/dog/dog_wolf_attachment.pdf
3. **D.G. Friedman, J.A. King, O. Elliot:** Critical Period in the Social Development of Dogs Science, March 1961

4 Influencing growth and development

1. **R.I. Krontveit, C. Trangerud, B.K. Sævik, H.K. Skogmo, A. Nødtvedt:** Risk factors for hip-related clinical signs in a prospective cohort study of four large dog breeds in Norway Preventative Veterinary Medicine, February 2012

5 Feeding your puppy

1. **The World Small Animal Veterinary Association:** Nutritional Assessment Guidelines www.wsava.org/sites/default/files/WSAVA%20Global%20Nutritional%20Assessment%20Guidelines%202011%20final.pdf
2. **Malathi Raghaven:** Diet related risk factors for gastric dilation-volvulus in dogs of high-risk breeds docs.lib.purdue.edu/dissertations/AAI3099198/
3. **L.T. Glickman, N.W. Glickman, C.M. Pérez, D.B. Schellenberg, G.C. Lantz:** Analysis of risk factors for gastric dilatation and dilatation-volvulus in dogs Journal of the American Veterinary Medical Association, May 1994
4. **L.T. Glickman, N.W. Glickman, D.B. Schellenberg, M. Raghaven, T. Lee:** Non-dietary risk factors for gastric

dilatation-volvulus in large and giant breed dogs Journal of the American Veterinary Medical Association, 2012

5. **M. Pipan, D.C. Brown, C.L. Battaglia, C.M. Otto:** An Internet-based survey of risk factors for surgical gastric dilatation-volvulus in dogs Journal of the American Veterinary Medical Association, 2012

6. **Royal Veterinary College:** Veterinary Periodontal Disease www.rvc.ac.uk/review/dentistry/shared_media/pdfs/perio_print.pdf

7. **Food and Drug Administration Pet Food Recalls 2013:** www.fda.gov/AnimalVeterinary/SafetyHealth/Recalls-Withdrawals/default.htm

6 Healthcare

1. **D.S. Edwards, W.E. Henley, J.L. Wood:** Vaccination and ill-health in dogs: a lack of temporal association and evidence of equivalence, Animal Health Trust, 2004

2. **L. Larson, S. Wynn, R.D. Schultz:** A Canine Parvovirus Nosode Study, Proceedings of the Second Annual Midwest Holistic Veterinary Conference, 1996

3. **G.E. Moore, L.F. Guptill, M.P. Ward, N.W. Glickman, K.K. Faunt, H.B. Lewis, L.T. Glickman:** Adverse events diagnosed within three days of vaccine administration in dogs. Proceedings of the Second Annual Midwest Holistic Veterinary Conference, 1996

4. **World Small Animal Veterinary Association:** Guidelines for the vaccination of dogs and cats www.wsava.org/sites/default/files/VaccinationGuidelines2010.pdf

5. **Veterinary Medicines Directorate** position paper on authorised vaccine schedules for dogs www.vmd.defra.gov.uk/pdf/vaccines_VMDpositionpaper.pdf

8 Puppy paperwork

1. **The Kennel Club:** What to expect from a breeder www.thekennelclub.org.uk/item/2101

14 Out and about

1. **American Veterinary Society of Animal Behavior:** Position statement on puppy socialisation avsabonline.org/uploads/position_statements/puppy_socialization.pdf

15 Beginning the puppy recall

1. **Pippa Mattinson:** Total Recall, Quiller, 2012

17 Biting and growling

1. **Ian Dunbar:** Before and After Getting Your Puppy, New World Library, 2004

18 Communication and bonding

1. **Victoria Stillwell:** Train Your Dog Positively, Ten Speed Press, 2013

20 Towards obedience

1. **Morgan Spector:** Clicker Training for Obedience, Sunshine Books 1999

2. **Karen Pryor:** Clicker Training for Dogs, Ringpress Books, 2002

23 Horrible habits

1. **Ben Hart:** Canine Conspecific Coprophagia: When, Who and Why Dogs Eat Stools American College of Veterinary Behaviorists/American Veterinary Society of Animal Behavior, 2012 symposium

24 Guarding food

1. **Jean Donaldson:** Oh Behave, Dogwise Publishing, 2008

25 Switching to raw feeding

1. **Tom Lonsdale:** Raw Meaty Bones, Rivetco Pty Ltd, 2001

26 Neutering and sexual maturity

1. **J.M. Hoffman, K.E. Creevy, D. Promislow:** Reproductive capability is associated with lifespan and cause of death in companion dogs PLOSone, April 2013 www.plosone.org
2. **J.M. Evans and Kay White:** The Book of The Bitch, Ringpress Books, revised edition, 2002
3. **R. Hagman:** New Aspects of Canine Pyometra, Studies on Epidemiology and Pathogenesis pub.epsilon.slu.se/736/1/Avhandlingsramen_f%C3%B6r_n%C3%A4rpublikation_R.Hagman.pdf
4. **Chris Zink DVM:** Early Spay–Neuter Considerations for the Canine Athlete: One Veterinarian's Opinion 2005 www.caninesports.com/uploads/1/5/3/1/15319800/spay_neuter_considerations_2013.pdf
5. **Lisa M. Howe, DVM:** Rebuttal to 'Early Spay–Neuter Considerations for the Canine Athlete'. www.columbusdogconnection.com/Documents/PedRebuttal%20.pdf
6. **A. Egenvall, R. Hagman, B.N. Bonnett, A. Hedhammar, P. Olson, A.S. Lagerstedt:** Breed risk of pyometra in insured dogs in Sweden Journal of Veterinary Internal Medicine, December 2001. www.onlinelibrary.wiley.com/journal
7. **Association of Animal Behaviour Professionals:** Effects of spaying and neutering on canine behaviour www.associationofanimalbehaviourprofessionals.com/effects_of_neutering.html
8. **J.C. Neilson, R.A. Eckstein, B.L. Hart:** Effects of castration on problem behaviours in male dogs with reference to age and duration of behaviour Journal of the American Veterinary Medical Association, July 1997

27 The disobedient puppy

1. **Jean Donaldson:** The Culture Clash, James and Kenneth Publishers, 1996
2. **Jane Killion:** When Pigs Fly, Dogwise Publishing, 2007

Further resources

The Kennel Club, 1–5 Clarges Street, Piccadilly, London W1J 8AB
Registering body for pedigree dogs in the UK, information on health, breeders and much more. www.thekennelclub.org.uk

The Gundog Club, Hearn Farm, Spats Lane, Headley, Hants GU35 8SU
Provides Graded Training Scheme for pet and working gundogs in the UK. Part of the Gundog Trust. www.thegundogclub.co.uk

The author's websites
The Labrador Site
Information on Labrador health, training, behaviour, raising puppies
www.thelabradorsite.com

Totally Dog Training
Information and resources for anyone wishing to train a dog
www.totallydogtraining.com

Youtube Training Videos
Pippa provides a number of dog training videos at
www.youtube.com/TheLabradorSite

🐾 Index